DON'T SHOOT THE CUSTOMER

Shocking Revelations About Customer Service

KEN NIETENHOEFER

JELM MOUNTAIN PUBLISHING
Laramie, Wyoming

Jelm Mountain Publishing
Laramie, Wyoming 82070

Additional books by Ken Nietenhoefer include the following:

50 Ways to Enrich Your Life, Book I

50 Ways to Enrich Your Life, Book II

Printed in the United States of America.
First printing 1996.

Although the author and publisher have made every effort to ensure the accuracy and completeness of information contained in this book, we assume no responsibility for errors, inaccuracies, omissions, or any inconsistency herein. Any slights of people, places, or organizations are unintentional.

Library of Congress Catalog Number: 95-092527
ISBN: 0-936204-52-4

ATTENTION COLLEGES AND UNIVERSITIES, CORPORATIONS AND PROFESSIONAL ORGANIZATIONS: Quantity discounts are available on bulk purchases of this book for educational training purposes, fund raising, or gift giving. For information call 1-800-756-9438.

ACKNOWLEDGEMENTS

It takes a combination of many people and numerous events to make a book like this possible. Over a two year period I obtained ideas, data, and experiences from a multitude of sources, and I am grateful for them all - even the not-so-pleasant ones.

I want to express my gratitude to the seventy-two corporations, associations, and other organizations that participated in the survey (listed in Appendix I), and especially to the ten outstanding organizations that I personally interviewed. They are featured in Chapter 8 and are listed below.

AAA Potomac
Amoco Oil Company
Bass Pro Shops
Brown and Sharpe Manufacturing Company
The Copps Corporation
Diamond Shamrock, Inc.
Federal Express
Gerber Products Company
The H. R. Chally Group
Marriott - San Antonio

I also want to thank all of the suppliers and sub-contractors that are so vital to my home-building business. My gratitude also goes out to Ms. Charlene

Maytum, my executive assistant, for helping me carry the load, as well as to my wife, Carol, for encouraging me even while I was simultaneously ignoring her and focusing on this book.

Special thanks also go out to Ms. Tiffany Hudkins, who put all of my ideas on paper and to Mr. Jay Hudkins for editing my words. Without these two fine individuals, this book would still be scribbled on pieces of notebook paper.

Most of all, however, I thank customers everywhere, the lifeblood of all business.

FOREWORD

"Old Man" McDaniel, as they called him in those days, never figured out what he'd been doing wrong all those years. I mean, despite the fact that he raised the finest horses anyone had ever laid eyes on, he just didn't seem able to make any money at it.

Buyers used to come from miles around just to look at his horses and they hoped they could convince the "Old Man" to sell them some of his stock. The fact was, he really needed to sell some of his horses each year to earn the required cash to buy the studs he needed to keep his breeding program going.

The truth was, he wanted to sell some of his stock to those buyers, but they showed up at the most inopportune times, they stayed longer than he wanted them to, and they even had the audacity to offer him less for his horses than he knew they were worth. That really irritated him!

As a matter of fact, sometimes he would become so irate that he chased them off his land, cursed them for coming, and even shot a few of them dead. The law was scarce in the territory in those days, so the "Old Man" was never convicted, nor even charged with a crime for that matter, but his reputation spread like wildfire throughout the region.

Every year, fewer potential buyers showed up, and that made him even angrier. The nerve! What in the hell was wrong with these people? Everyone knew he had the finest horses available, so why would they even question his prices? They had no right to leave empty-handed. He figured he had to teach them a lesson, that was all that there was to it.

Well, as one might guess, times became tougher and tougher for the "Old Man" until one day the bank took his land, his pride, and his horses. He just simply couldn't understand what had gone wrong.

Hadn't he always worked hard? Hadn't he always had the best stock available? Hadn't he always had what everybody wanted? What rotten luck! Should've shot every last one of them. That would've taught 'em a lesson.

Trouble is, he never learned his lesson: "You can't shoot the customer and expect to survive."

TABLE OF CONTENTS

INTRODUCTION

Most of us would readily agree that the "Old Man" in the foregoing story was utterly insensitive, ignorant, and stupid. After all, no one in his or her right mind would act like that. Right? Wrong! It happens every day - maybe not literally, but certainly figuratively.

Fred Smith, founder of Federal Express, sums it up rather well: "The U.S. has been terrible as it applies to customer service. I mean, we killed the goose that laid the golden egg. Somehow, management let employees believe that customers weren't important."

The Harvard Business Review says, "Daily we encounter inattention to quality - overemphasis on scale economics rather than on customers' concerns. Too many service companies have concentrated on cost-cutting efficiencies they can quantify, rather than on adding to their products' value by listening carefully and providing service their customers genuinely want."

So, there you have it. I'll bet you can recall several incidents in which you were a victim of poor customer service. Not only that, but I'll bet you told your friends and co-workers about those incidents, too.

That's the problem, isn't it? Just like it did in the story about the "Old Man," bad news travels fast, and if you're the one providing poor customer service, the rumors will return to haunt you.

* * * * * * * *

This book will discuss the customer service industry as a whole - its history, show why it is so important, and discuss how we are presently doing. You will develop a new mindset regarding the term "service." No longer will you equate it with "servitude."

We will redefine the word "customer" to include not only the ultimate consumer, but also the internal customers -- employees, co-workers, vendors, department heads, managers, etc. We will expand the term to include our students, our friends, and our children -- especially our children.

You will discover that not only will you no longer have to put up with rude, insensitive service providers, but also how to go about severing your ties and taking your business elsewhere.

We will delve into the future of customer service. How can we develop effective service strategies, customer relations, and employee satisfaction? I will introduce you to my G.U.N.S. program and then explore the relationship between Total Quality Management (TQM), Total Customer Focus (TCF), and customer service.

No program, no matter how well thought out, is complete without effective communications. We cannot be human alone. I will introduce you to my "DARE to Communicate" program, as well as the importance of effective listening - including "hearing versus listening," the benefits of listening, and the obstacles to effective listening.

At this point, you will have been exposed to the basic concepts concerning customer service and its significance to your success or failure. To add flavoring to the meat, I will share with you the results of a nationwide customer service survey that we have been conducting during the past year or so. The results are, in some cases surprising, and in some cases -- even shocking! But in all cases, they are fascinating.

Then, it really gets interesting. Where most books stop, this one starts. Since I own several businesses, including two custom home building companies, I am in a unique position not only to talk about the concepts and theories of customer service, but also to share my personal experiences with you. You'll discover, as I did, that talking about customer service is one thing, but doing it is another.

Now that we've added flavoring, we will add hot pepper. I believe schools' customers are their students, alumni, parents, and townspeople. I believe the government's customers are its people and it should be of service to those it serves. I believe parents' customers are their children and if we don't guide, discipline, and nurture them, we are doing them a gross disservice. Wow! What next? Read on.

The last chapter will include several of my columns which relate to customer service as they appeared in the newspaper.

Now, as you prepare to read on, keep in mind that our customers are our lifeblood. Don't shoot 'em.

1 CHANGING THE MINDSET

There seems to be a gross misconception as it applies to the word "service"--i.e., many equate "service" with "servitude". Nothing could be further from the truth.

The misconception surrounding the service business probably grew from the fact that, originally, service was performed primarily by unskilled personnel. For example, housekeepers, janitors, street sweepers, shoe-shine boys, and yard-keepers were the first service-oriented people. They were generally regarded as being uneducated, underprivileged, and lacking in real ambition.

As a result, they were relegated to a lower class in our society, not the type of people with whom the average white collar worker would normally associate--especially in a social setting. They were, in the eyes of many (especially the snootier folks), not much better than slaves.

Isn't it amazing just how hypocritical a society can be? These "service-type" people were simply not the kind of people with whom one would want to have a drink, attend parties, or (heaven forbid!) marry. Is it any wonder, then, that "service" is sometimes still associated with "servitude?"

As time progressed and our society became more sophisticated, the demand for additional services grew. Working people, which included an increasing number of women, simply found themselves running out of time (and expertise) to take care of all their needs and problems.

Industrialization and trade increased, thereby opening opportunities for real entrepreneurs. Needs developed for storekeepers, merchants, repair people, and maintenance experts, not to mention the desire for additional governmental services.

As our society grew in numbers and in complexity, it required even more services to be performed. Accountants were needed because our tax laws became too complex for the average wage earner to understand. Legal services were needed because our elected officials failed to simplify things. Insurance companies blossomed because we became a litigious society, medical costs spiraled grotesquely, and the masses longed for some sort of security.

Now that we have entered the "information age," services are becoming increasingly important. The average person is bombarded incessantly with so many facts, figures, and ideas that one cannot possibly comprehend even a fraction of what one must in order to survive.

Consequently, we need help--specialized help. Imagine what it would be like if we had no hotels, airlines, car rental agencies, restaurants, take-home meals, pool-cleaning services, car-washing and lubrication stations, traffic reports on the radio, newspapers and information magazines, electricity, or dieting services.

It is evident, then, that as a society increases in wealth and sophistication, demand for services will increasingly outweigh the demand for commodities. The populace will become increasingly specialized; thus, as one gets to know more about less, one will know less about more. Hence, the need for specialized services will undoubtedly grow at an exponential rate.

We simply cannot be expected to be experts at cooking, auto maintenance, child-raising, computer programming, real estate, tax consequences, home-building, labor relations, law, or school politics--all at the same time. We need experts in these and thousands of other jobs to help, guide, and aid us. If one insists on doing everything, one will, at best, do a half-way decent job on any of them, and maybe even become a blubbering idiot with no focus and little effectiveness.

Already, 60 percent of the population in the United States is involved in the service business; by the year 2000, it is estimated that 88 percent will be. Two-thirds of our gross national product is created by the service industry. Of all the new companies which will be started during the 90's, 80 percent will be service companies.

According to J. Michael Farr, in his book America's 50 Fastest Growing Jobs, and the U.S Department of Labor statistics, 4 out of every 5 jobs by the year 2000 will be in the service sector. Table I below illustrates the 50 fastest growing jobs and their projected percentage of growth.

THE TOP 50 FASTEST GROWING JOBS				
	Occupation	% Growth Projected	Numerical Growth	Estimated Total Employment 1988
1.	Paralegals	75	62,000	83,000
2.	Medical Assistants	70	104,000	149,000
3.	Radiological Technologists	66	87,000	132,000
4.	Homemaker-Home Health Aides	63	207,000	327,000
5.	Medical Record Technicians	60	28,000	47,000
6.	Medical Secretaries	58	120,000	207,000
7.	Physical Therapists	57	39,000	68,000
8.	Surgical Technologists	56	20,000	35,000
9.	Securities and Financial Services Representatives	55	109,000	200,000
10.	Operations Research Analysts	55	30,000	55,000
11.	Travel Agents	54	77,000	142,000
12.	Actuaries	54	8,500	16,000
13.	Computer System Analysts	53	214,000	402,000
14.	Physical and Corrective Therapy Assistants	52.5	21,000	39,000
15.	Social Welfare Service Aides	51.5	47,000	91,000
16.	EEG Technologists	50	3,200	6,400
17.	Occupational Therapists	49	16,000	33,000
18.	Computer Programmers	48	250,000	519,000
19.	Service Sales Representatives	45	216,000	481,000
20.	Human Services Workers	45	53,000	118,000
21.	Health Services Managers	42	75,000	177,000

22.	Corrections Officers	41	76,000	186,000
23.	Respiratory Therapists	41	23,000	56,000
24.	Receptionists	40	331,000	833,000
25.	Electrical and Electronics Engineers	40	176,000	439,000
26.	Employment Interviewers	40	33,000	81,000
27.	Registered Nurses	39	613,000	1,577,000
28.	Flight Attendants	39	34,000	88,000
29.	Licensed Practical Nurses	37	229,000	626,000
30.	Recreational Therapists	37	9,500	26,000
31.	Management Analysts and Consultants	35	46,000	130,000
32.	Computer and Office Machine Repairers	35	44,000	128,000
33.	Podiatrists	35	5,700	17,000
34.	Information Clerks	34	441,000	1,316,000
35.	Guards	32	256,000	795,000
36.	Engineering, Science, and Data Processing Managers.	32	83,000	258,000
37.	Nursing Aides and Psychiatric Aides	31	405,000	1,298,000
38.	Aircraft Pilots	31	26,000	83,000
39.	Dispensing Opticians	31	16,000	49,000
40.	Lawyers and Judges	30	188,000	622,000
41.	Childcare Workers	30	186,000	670,000
42.	Actors, Directors, and Producers	30	24,000	80,000
43.	Nuclear Medicine Technologists	30	3,000	10,000
44.	Meteorologists	30	1,800	6,200
45.	Social Workers	29	110,000	385,000
46.	Computer and Peripheral Equip. Operators	29	92,000	316,000

47.	Underwriters	29	30,000	103,000
48.	Landscape Architects	29	5,500	19,000
49.	Engineering Technicians	28	203,000	722,000
50.	Physicians	28	149,000	535,000

Yet, perception of the service industry remains skewed. It reminds one of a story about a first-grader named Jimmy. His mother told him she was about to give him a new baby brother. He was so thrilled that he talked about nothing else every day at school, so much, in fact, that his teacher and classmates grew weary of listening to him rant and rave about his new baby brother.

One morning, just before Jimmy was ready to leave for school, his mother said, "Jimmy! Would you like to feel your baby brother kicking? Come here and feel my tummy and you can feel him kick."

Jimmy put his hand on his mother's tummy, and sure enough, he felt his baby brother kicking. He had the most quizzical, confused look on his face because he didn't know what to think about all this.

That day at school, Jimmy didn't utter a word about his baby brother. His teacher couldn't understand why; after all, that's all Jimmy had been talking about for the past several weeks. So, before he left to go home, his teacher asked him, "Jimmy, you haven't said a word about your baby brother today?" Why not?" Jimmy replied, "I think my mommy ate 'im."

Just as Jimmy harbored a gross misconception about the conditions surrounding the impending birth of his baby brother, many of us also harbor gross misconceptions about the service business. Some still consider the service segment of our economy as the sales and the manufacturing segment the real "meat of the meal."

However, as early as 1981, Paul Hawkin boldly proclaimed the decline of the "mass economy" and the rise of the "informative economy" in his book The Next Economy. He observed that:

> *"We are witnessing the relative decline of what I call the mass economy, the economy of the industrial age, a period during which nations amassed enormous manufacturing capabilities that depended on the large-scale extraction of resources, particularly fossil fuels.*
>
> *The mass economy was a formative economy in which virtually all of the work that human beings once did by hand or with the assistance of animals became mechanized through the use of machinery, technology, and energy. This mechanization included the development of the automobile, steel, rubber, chemical, electrical, heavy equipment, and machine tool industries as well as the thousands of businesses required to support them."*

By no means am I minimizing the importance nor the impact of the manufacturing segment of our economy. Indeed, it would be a sad day for this country if we completely discontinued manufacturing goods and, instead, only provided services. Soon, there wouldn't be anyone left for whom to provide those services.

What I am suggesting, however, is that we must recognize the impact and the importance of the service segment of our economy. Only then will we be able to take full advantage of the concept and cash in on the vast opportunities which are available to us.

Some of you have already taken advantage of this inevitable trend; others are still considering it. Every day, we hear of people who lost their jobs and were forced to engage in alternate work. Similarly, we hear of people who became burned out in large corporations and escaped to secluded locations, only to create new opportunities for themselves and for others.

I recently met a former home builder who now cleans houses and yards--and is happier and better off financially than he was as a home builder. On a personal note, during the economic downturn of the late 80's, no one could afford to build a new home. As a result, and in order to survive, I became heavily involved in the energy-saving business, retro-fitting older homes and offices with energy-saving material. The move helped me survive, saved my customers substantial amounts on their electric bills, and paved the way for my company to thrive once the economy returned to normal.

The irony of the situation is that I still offer the same energy-saving material to my clients today. It saves them money and makes me money.

It does require a change in our mind-set, however, to take full advantage of trends in our economy. You can either live in the past and lament the passing of the "good old days," or you can grab hold of the opportunities afforded. The choice is yours.

To help you make that choice, to help you really understand the service, to help you realize the importance of excellent customer service (providing it and receiving it), those are the purposes for which this book is written. So return your gun to your holster before you shoot yourself in the foot. But more important than that, **DON'T SHOOT THE CUSTOMER!**

HOW ARE WE DOING?

Unfortunately, not very well. As I quoted in the Introduction, Fred Smith, founder of Federal Express, believes the U.S. has been terrible as it applies to customer service. The Harvard Business Review accuses us of concentrating on cost-cutting efficiencies we can quantify, rather that on adding to our products' value by listening carefully and providing services our customers genuinely want.

In the educational realm, a report by The Wingspread Group on Higher Education entitled An American Imperative: Higher Expectations for Higher Education, the consensus is negative. It reports that, "Like much of the rest of American education, the nation's colleges and universities appear to live by an unconscious educational rule of thumb that their function is to weed out, not to cultivate, students for whom they have accepted responsibility."

But the problem is not confined only to our nation's universities. According to the January 27, 1994 edition of The Wall Street Journal, "The No. 3 auto maker (Chrysler) has the worst quality record of Detroit's Big Three, as determined by J.D. Power and Associates' annual initial quality survey" (Not to mention how poorly the company fared as compared to its Japanese counterparts).

Furthermore, our judicial system is wallowing in mediocrity and is increasingly demonstrating its ineffectiveness. Every night, fearful northern Denver residents, as well as many other city dwellers, lock themselves in their homes as their streets become battlefields in an escalating gang war. Courts everywhere are failing to serve their customers by handling even convicted felons with kid gloves. As I write this book, the news constantly reports about the latest gang-related shooting in San Antonio.

The U.S. Chamber of Commerce is coming under fire from many of its members (those whom it is supposed to serve) for considering backing the kind of employer mandate proposed in President Clinton's health-care reform bill. Then, in a "brilliant" move after scores of members complained to the national headquarters, the chamber reversed its stance on employer mandates, ordered a poll of its members on health-care reform, and recently fired its top lobbyist in a major staff shake-up.

T.A.R.P. RESEARCH

There are numerous additional examples one could mention, but let me summarize by referring to the study performed by the Technical Assistance Research Programs Institute (T.A.R.P.) for member agencies of the Consumer Affairs Council at the request of the United States Office of Consumer Affairs. Its general findings are below.

1. Many American households experience consumer problems:
    - 32.4 percent of households experienced a problem.
    - Approximately one out of four purchases resulted in some type of consumer problem experience.
2. Many consumers who experience problems with products or services do not complain:
    - 31 percent of the problem households did not complain about their most serious problem.
    - Nearly 70 percent of those experiencing a problem did not complain.
3. Most complaints are registered at the place where the product was bought or where the service was received:
    - 87.3 percent of initial complaints were registered at the point of purchase.

- Fewer than five percent of the complaints about large ticket durable goods or services ever reach the manufacturer.

4. Several factors influence consumer complaint behavior:
    - Consumers experiencing severe problems are more likely to complain than those encountering minor ones.
    - High income households are more likely to complain than low income households.
    - The young are more likely to complain than the elderly.
    - Northeastern households (especially New York) report disproportionately high complaint submission rates.
5. There are three principle reasons why consumers who experience product or service problems do not complain:
    - Complaining wasn't worth their time or effort.
    - They didn't know how or where to complain.
    - They believed complaining wouldn't do any good; no one wanted to hear about their problems.
6. Many complainants are not satisfied with the action taken by business to resolve their problems. There is a strong relationship

between problem severity and complainant dissatisfaction. The more severe the consumer problem, the lower the level of complainant satisfaction.

Well, that is probably enough statistical data to convince you that we have a customer service problem in this country. The most meaningful statistic, however, is you. How many of you have ever been a victim of lousy customer service? My point is made.

WHY IS CUSTOMER SERVICE IMPORTANT?

It's an interesting question. Even though thousands of books and articles have been written about how to improve customer service, it might be interesting to discuss the importance of the subject. Is it all that important? Why is it all that important? Here goes---

There are THREE GENERALLY ACCEPTED REASONS for the importance of exhibiting excellent customer service:

REASON #1: One out of four of your customers is unhappy enough to leave you! (and 90% of those will).

Why do they leave?

1% die
3% move
5% develop other friendships
9% actually find a cheaper price

14% are dissatisfied with your product/service

BUT--68% LEAVE BECAUSE OF AN ATTITUDE OF INDIFFERENCE.

That's the bad news, but it gets worse. The average victim of poor customer service will tell 10 others about his or her experience. The following example will illustrate how devastating this phenomenon can be:

1. Assume a business has 100 customers
2. One out of four is unhappy enough to leave (25 customers)
3. They tell 10 other people

25 unhappy customers		
X 10 people told	**250**	negative customers
plus the	**25**	original unhappy customers
Total	**275**	negative customers or 275 people aware of poor customer service

The happy customers only tell one other person about their experience.

75 happy customers X 1 person told	**75**	positive customers
plus the 75 original customers	**75**	positive customers

Total **150** positive units or 150 people aware of positive customer service

So there you have it, **275 dissatisfied people** and only **150 satisfied people**. Where does it look like we're going? Downhill, right? In a hurry!

One would reasonably assume most customers would complain loudly and the problem would immediately be rectified. Not so.

The fact is, most of us elect to say nothing, and instead we slink away without saying a word and we simply take our business elsewhere. Why aren't customers more vocal?

First, they don't think it's worth the effort. Second, they don't know where or how to complain. Third, they figure that the company won't do anything about the complaint anyway. Pretty sad, isn't it?

REASON #2: It costs six times more to attract new customers and clients than it does to keep the present ones. Just consider all the marketing efforts which go into developing strategies to attract new customers. Millions of dollars are spent (perhaps wasted) on a wide array of media advertising and in may cases its effects are negated at the "moment of truth," the instant of actual contact a customer makes with the company.

Carl Sewell, car dealer and author of Customers for Life, exhorts us to treat customers like appreciating assets. Don't consider them as one-time events, but rather as life-long partners.

Most of you are aware that sales people are paid commissions. They normally receive all, or at least the majority of, their money when they make the sale. Is it any wonder, then, that sales people must satisfy their customers completely to make a sale and to receive their money?

Case in point: Why do insurance agents receive most of their commissions when they make the sale and only a dribble as time wears on? What normally happens? They concentrate not on servicing their regular, steady clients, but on generating new business. In many cases, as a result, they lose their regular clients due to an attitude of indifference or disinterest.

REASON #3: Excellent customer service used to be regarded as a "necessary evil," an expense, but now we know that it increases sales and reduces the cost of sales. Even the most hard-hearted business person can recognize the merit of this phenomenon.

Businesses with perceived poor customer service:

- Average 1% return on sales
- Lose 2% of market share each year

Businesses with perceived excellent customer service:

- Average 12% return on sales
- Gain 6% of market share each year

Where would you rather be? For which type of company would you rather work? Where would you rather do business?

ADDITIONAL REASONS MAKING CUSTOMER SERVICE IMPORTANT:

TARP (Technical Assistance Research Programs) recently issued a report entitled "Trends That Create a Need For Improved Customer Service." The report cites eight major trends which create a need for better-trained, more sensitive service representatives.

1. Failure of customers to read. For instance, Polaroid and Whirlpool found that up to 30 percent of all warranty repairs and service visits were made because the customer failed to fully understand the product.
2. Delegation of responsibility back to the customer. Many companies, in an effort to cut costs, are requiring customers to assemble and maintain the product themselves.
3. More high tech and product complexity makes products undifferentiable. Consequently, the key attributes which differentiate products are service and recommendations of friends.
4. Lower confidence and expectations regarding products and services. Therefore, companies which give better service will differentiate themselves from their competitors.

5. Use of high quality service in advertising. If a company uses this method, it better be able to follow through with excellent service.

6. Media attention. The media has found that highlighting consumer difficulties is a popular news item.

7. Rising prices and service charges. Consumers' perceived price/value ratio for most products is going down; they believe they are receiving less for their money.

8. Recognition of costs of turnover and negative environments for workers. The implication is that corporations are attempting to reduce burnout and employee dissatisfaction.

Enough reasons?

IN SUMMARY: Excellent customer service is more than a competitive weapon; it's a survival skill. It's not just a competitive edge; it's THE competitive edge.

2 HISTORY - THEIRS AND MINE

One would think that with all the talk about customer service in books, magazines, news articles, seminars, radio, television, and cute slogans, almost everyone would be keenly aware of, and turned on to, providing excellent customer service. It's almost impossible today to go anywhere without being reminded about the importance of treating the customer right.

For decades, most larger companies have had customer service departments whose job was to field customer complaints, and hopefully, satisfy customers' needs. For a long time, slogans, smile-training, posters, and buttons have proliferated the American business scene.

"Then why," you might ask, "do we need yet another book dealing with this subject?" It's a darn good question because theoretically, at least, there are more than enough good books on the subject already. So what's the problem? The problem is two-fold as I see it: First, the people who should be reading them, aren't; and, second, those who are reading them aren't doing what the books say they should be doing.

I really believe the first reason is the major culprit. Too many books which have been written on the subject are written with only the business person in mind. As a result, the books end up in the business sections in book stores and many people aren't even aware the books exist. In other cases, the books are technically-oriented and aren't all that easy to read.

Consequently, because of the knowledge I've gained by presenting customer service seminars, writing columns and articles on the subject, and my personal experiences as a consumer in the marketplace, I decided there was a real need for a "reader-friendly" customer service book. That's what this book is.

There is definitely a real need for books of this type. If you don't believe that, wait until you read this chapter. Then decide for yourself.

The purpose of this chapter is to convince you that even though millions of words have been written about the importance of providing excellent customer service, they haven't had much of an impact. Unfortunately, poor customer service is the rule instead of the exception.

How many times have you been verbally stepped on, slapped down, side-swiped, or even worse, ignored? How many times have you wished that somehow you could get even with someone who mistreated you? More than you can remember?

YOU AREN'T THE ONLY ONE.

The United States Office of Consumer Affairs (USOCA) contracted with the Technical Assistance Research Programs Institute (TARP) to conduct an updated "Study of Consumer Complaints by Government, Business and Voluntary Complaint Handling in America." The updated study in 1984 had two objectives:

1.. To provide an overview of the changes since the 1974-79 national study.

2. To recognize recent findings on consumer behavior to provide specific recommendations for action by government, business, voluntary groups, and individual
citizens.

WHAT DID THE STUDY FIND?

1. Many American households experience consumer problems:

- 32.4 percent of households experienced a problem.

- Approximately one out of four purchases resulted in some type of consumer problem experience.

2. Many consumers who experience problems with products or services do not complain:

- 31 percent of the problem households did not complain about their most serious problem.
- Nearly 70 percent of those experiencing a problem did not complain.

3. Fewer than five percent of the complaints about large ticket durable goods or services ever reach the manufacturer.

4. Many complainants are not satisfied with the action taken by business to resolve their problems.

5. The average business never hears from 96 percent of its unhappy customers.

6. The average unhappy customer will tell 9 or 10 other people about his or her experience. Thirteen percent will tell up to 20 others about it.

7. One out of four customers are unhappy enough to leave (90% of those will).

8. It costs six times more to attract new customers and clients than to keep the present ones.

OTHER STUDIES

In the September 3, 1990 issue of Industry Week, David Altany wrote an article entitled "One Step Beyond Customer Satisfaction." In it, he states, "The race to please customers is on, winner take all."

He goes on to say that, "in fact, competition in mature industries is heating up to the point that companies are finding that `just' satisfying customers is only an intermediate goal, a prerequisite to staying in business. To prosper, and to differentiate themselves from competitors, companies are discovering that they must reach beyond customer satisfaction."

So where's the rub? He continues: "Despite impressive gains by leading-edge companies, though, the importance of becoming customer-oriented remains a mystery to many product-oriented manufacturers. Some cling to the notion that consumers buy solely on the basis of product quality. They are unaware of the extent to which consumers are influenced by past experiences, by the pleasantness of sales and support staffs, and by the promise of responsive and committed service after the purchase."

SOUR SMELL

Dan Richards, in his article "Sour Smell of Poor Customer Service" in the December 28, 1992 issue of the Wall Street Journal, reminds us that there is a "remarkable chasm between these head-office professions of commitment to the customer and the actual behavior toward those self-same customers down the line."

And why are so many employees non-responsive? "Often, they've lived with the smell of poor customer service for so long that they don't notice it anymore," says Richards.

VISION FAILS

In the 1991 November-December issue of the Harvard Business Review, Ron Zempke writes, "Time and again we have seen service quality improvement efforts flounder because senior management failed to communicate clearly its vision of quality service."

In the same article, Walter F. Loeb states, "Most of the service industry is out of touch with society. Too many companies fail to create excitement and a feeling of belonging for employees."

RETAIL INDUSTRY GROWS IMPERSONAL

Charles E. Cox, in the March 1992 issue of HR Magazine, reminds us that "The level of customer service provided by retail stores today is actually the result of forces that have evolved over a period of years. The so-called carriage-trade department stores, locally owned and operated by some of this country's finest entrepreneurs, understood customer service and provided it so well they inspired intense customer loyalty."

"One by one these entrepreneurial stores have been replaced by impersonal corporate entities, and customer-oriented policies and procedures have eroded in favor of tight expense control, and a fixation on bottom-line profitability, short-term growth and unrestrained expansion," he says.

MEDIOCRE SERVICE

Ron Zempke, in the January 1992 issue of Training, depresses us with this reminder: "Most of us find out every day that service in North America is, at best, mediocre. The pages of the daily newspaper are filled with titillating tidbits about bad service:

> *Airlines can't get you there safely, on time, with your luggage intact. Fix-it shops can't fix it, and they blame you for expecting them to.*
>
> *Hospitals treat patients like meat. Restaurants treat diners like mental patients. Banks tell you, "Put it in the mail or use the money wall or phone it in, but don't talk to me, pal, I'm too important to deal with customers."*

CHARTING THE ISSUES

Management Review, in its December 1990 issue, reports the results of an extensive American Management Association survey: Almost four-fifths, or 78 percent, say that improving customer service is the key to competitive success. And 92 percent believe that giving superior service is one of their key responsibilities, regardless of position.

But while individual respondents give high priority to customer service as a key to competitive advantage, they report that actual implementation of customer service lags behind the evident need. Only 56 percent say that service to the customer is a clear and accepted priority throughout the organization.

Only 22 percent of the respondents say their companies seriously analyze competitors. Less than half prepare regular reports on customer satisfaction, and a mere 44 percent "quickly eliminate bureaucracy" if it gets in the way of good customer service.

PERSONAL ENCOUNTERS WITH POOR CUSTOMER SERVICE

It is a safe bet that each one of you has experienced poor customer service and has shared those experiences with your friends, relatives, and neighbors. I invite you to share them with me by sending them to the address at the back of this book. Let me share some of mine with you.

NEW COMPUTER

My company had outgrown its computer, so we began shopping around for a newer, better one--which is very difficult to do when one is basically computer-illiterate. All I knew about computers was how to plug one in to the wall. Anyway, we contacted several dealers to see what they had to offer.

The first dealer showed up, showered us with facts and figures, but failed to speak in the very English language that we could understand. (To me, a megabyte was what a big dog likes to give to a mailman's butt).

In any case, he didn't impress us, so we waited for the second salesperson to show up. Not only were we able to speak to a salesperson, but we spoke to the sale's manager himself! "Computers Made Simple" was about to score a major victory.

Now we were really getting somewhere, I thought. He recommended some hardware for us, but he failed to mention any brand names. When I, in my naiveté, meekly asked about "name brands," he arrogantly proclaimed that the hardware was going to be CMS (Computers Made Simple).

Wow! I should have known--stupid me. In other words, he was going to put together a mix and match of parts depending on where he could buy them at the cheapest price, and then he would pawn the conglomeration off on me.

Finally, a young man came to our office for the purpose of actually helping us fill our needs. Guess where we purchased our new computer?

IN THE MOUNTAINS

A year ago, my wife and I traveled to Ruidoso, New Mexico, to relax in the mountains for a few days. One morning, we decided to eat breakfast at the local McDonalds. We walked into a crowded situation. The few tables which weren't occupied were dirty and desperately needed cleaning.

It appeared that one of the bus persons, or wait persons, had been asked to conduct a customer survey (hey, I thought it sounded like a good idea); but, unfortunately, she also had to perform her regular duties.

So there she was, attempting to survey customers, asking them how they enjoyed their food, drinks, etc.--instead of cleaning tables. That was the only thing anybody was interested in at the time--just finding a clean table at which to eat.

She obviously was not well-trained to conduct the survey, and management obviously had a one-track mind (conduct surveys), rather than ensuring that its customers were actually satisfied (with full tummies).

HOTEL INACTION

During a recent ski trip, my wife, my daughter, my son-in-law, and I rented a room at the Inn of the Mountain Gods near Ruidoso, New Mexico. We checked in and were getting ready to take our showers when we discovered we needed additional towels I called the front desk and requested the towels.

After an hour or so went by, we realized we had not yet received the additional towels which I had requested, so I called the front desk again. Yet another hour went by; we still had not received our additional towels.

Finally, my son-in-law, Steve, called the front desk to determine the status of our request. The agent on duty didn't have a clue as to what was going on.

Steve went to the front desk and personally asked the clerk to get him some towels, but she refused, saying it “was not her duty to do so.”

He then asked to speak with the hotel manager. The manager finally appeared and he offered an apology for the whole sorry incident. While this was taking place, additional towels had been delivered to our room.

By this time we didn't know whether to laugh or to just stay angry. There was a gross lack of coordination; but even worse, there prevailed a generally lousy attitude.

NEW TELEVISION

My wife and I were recently in the market to purchase a new television set, so we paid a visit to Sam's. We immediately spotted one we thought would fulfill our needs, but since we didn't have a tape measure with us, we weren't sure the set would physically fit into our cabinet.

But we were in luck. Right? There were two gentlemen moving other TV's, so we asked them if they knew the dimensions of the set in which we were interested. They answered with a simple "no." We then asked if either one of them had a tape measure so that we might measure the set. Once again, they replied, "no."

After we expressed our amazement that neither one of the gentleman would have a measuring tape, they explained to us that they used to carry measuring tapes, but customers borrowed them and failed to return them. (Hey, now we understood! Dumb us).

By this time, my wife was ready to find the manager, but I suggested we ask someone in another department if they had a measuring tape. We did, they did, and we measured the TV. (Oh, and we returned the tape, too).

We made it a point to inform the two men that the adjacent department did, in fact, have a measuring tape. We also made it a point to inform them that we wouldn't purchase this TV, or ANY TV, or ANYTHING AT ALL from their store. They didn't seem to care.

I could go on and on, and I'll bet you could, too, but I believe the point has been made. As I said earlier, despite all the rhetoric which has been written and spoken about the need for excellence in customer service, it is rare to actually witness it or experience it. Instead, it is more common to encounter the uncaring, the untrained, and the insensitive. That's the negative news.

There is, however, some positive news: YOU DON'T HAVE TO PUT UP WITH SORRY CUSTOMER SERVICE. Wow! What a revelation. YOU CAN, AND SHOULD, DEMAND EXCELLENT CUSTOMER SERVICE.

SO?! WHAT DOES IT MEAN?

So, how does one go about expecting, demanding, and receiving excellent customer service?

Simply put, take your business elsewhere if you don't receive it where you are now. Vote with your dollars.

Wouldn't it be great if we lived in a country where everyone voted? Well, the fact is, we do. Everyone votes everyday with his or her dollars. As consumers, we have the ultimate power. We can make or break a business. We can make it extremely uncomfortable even for the surly civil servant. We can vote out an unresponsive politician. In short, this is one instance where every vote counts. So do it!

3 FUTURE OF CUSTOMER SERVICE

What is the future of the concept of "customer service?" Is it merely a fad, or is it a continuing way of life?

Tim Clark, in the March 1993 issue of Business Marketing, refers to a survey by Plant Engineering and Ernst & Young: CEO's and plant managers of major U.S. manufacturing firms say customer service is the most important factor for remaining competitive in the 1990's.

USAA's Robert F. McDermott says, "The mission and corporate culture of this company are, in one word, service." Andrew H. Szpedman, in the September 1992 issue of HR Magazine says, "In buying for the same clientele--consumers face an array of hard-to-distinguish products that tout similar benefits.

Recognizing this, more organizations are focusing on quality of service to set themselves apart."

Karl Albrecht and Ron Zempke in Service America, preface their book by saying, "People are getting more and more critical of the quality of service they experience in their everyday lives, and they want something done about it. The times call for a new focus on service. . . . ". The quality of the customer's experience is becoming a hot topic in board rooms and executives' suites, not only in the United States but in many other countries as well."

What do you think? Have you experienced excellent customer service in your last several forays into the department store, city tax department, muffler shop, car dealership, or restaurant? Would you like to? There's the answer: The need for excellent customer service is not a current fad. Actually, it's a phenomenon which hasn't been around all that long and isn't generally being practiced as well as it should be right now. BUT IT NEEDS TO BE PRACTICED IN THE FUTURE.

In order to discuss the future of customer service, let's break it down into three aspects:

A. Service strategy.
B. The GUNS program
C. Total Customer Focus (TCF)

A. SERVICE STRATEGY

What is it? It is a distinctive formula for delivering service through vision. It answers these questions: What is the marketplace?, What is your position in that marketplace?, and What position do you want to occupy in that marketplace?

What are its ingredients?

1. Reliable market research and proper analysis. (An example: Johnny placed a call on the pay phone in the local drug store. "Mr. Jones, I understand that you need someone to cut your grass this summer. Oh, you say that you already have someone to cut your grass? I see. And how is he doing? You say he's doing very well. Is there anything that he could be doing better? So you are quite satisfied then? Okay, thanks anyway." The druggist, having overheard the conversation, inquired, "Johnny, aren't you taking care of Mr. Jones' yard?" Johnny replied, "Yes, I am, but I wanted to find out how I was doing."

2. A mission statement--(What makes you unique? What is your target market?) It is interesting to note the number of mission statements we received as a result of our

research. We will discuss them in a later chapter.

3. Clearly stated and well-publicized corporate principles which are the beliefs and values of the organization.

4. "Visible management"--it's a requisite today. It involves setting the example, especially in family life.

5. Total commitment--top to bottom. What does a service strategy do for you?

- It positions you in the marketplace.
- It provides direction for the organization.
- It lets front-line people know what's expected of them and what's important to the organization.

B. GUNS PROGRAM

No discussion of service strategy could be complete without a review of my GUNS program. Service strategy is basically an outgrowth of a certain mindset. An organization either exudes excellent customer service or it doesn't. It's that simple.

Figures 3-1 and 3-2 are visual presentations of my GUNS program. You will notice that each set of concentric boxes represents a certain type of organization: Box 1 represents a typical organization.

Box G (generic) is disproportionately large, thereby illustrating that this type of organization spends a disproportionate amount of time and money on items which should be part of the operation anyway.

Box U (usual) is somewhat smaller, but still too large. Too much energy is being expended on normal, usual aspects.

Box N (nice, or nifty) is smaller yet. This organization is not spending enough time, money, nor energy on the special aspects which could set it apart from others.

Box S (superb, super, SUCCESSFUL) is still smaller. Instead of emphasizing this special area, it is almost ignored.

Now, let's go to Box 2: This is an organization which emphasizes excellent customer service.

Box G (generic) is certainly important and is not ignored. However, it is also not over-emphasized.

Box U (usual) is also important, but is expected, a "given."

Box N (nice, nifty) is quite different than its counterpart in Figure 3-1. Notice how much additional emphasis is being placed on this aspect. This organization is beginning to differentiate itself from its counterpart.

Box S (superb, super, SUCCESSFUL) Wow! Look at the difference. While this organization bestows an adequate amount of energy, time and money on the inner boxes, it emphasizes the outer boxes. Thus, it is visibly different from the normal organization. It is also much more successful.

Figure 3-1

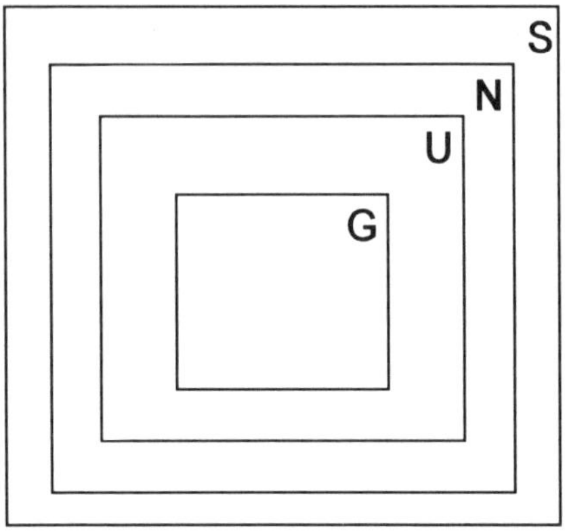

Figure 3-2

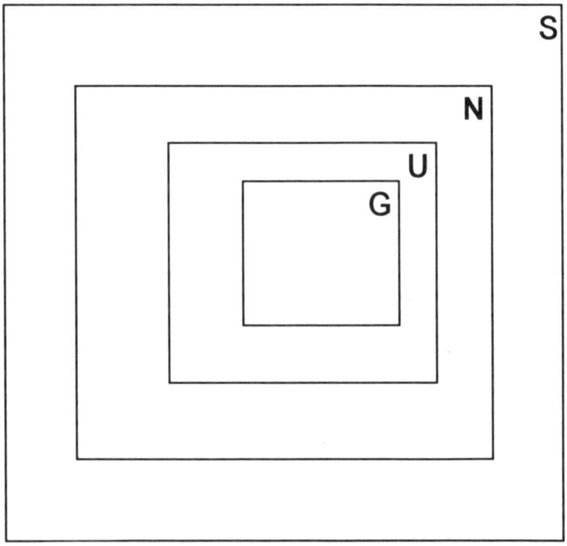

C. TOTAL CUSTOMER FOCUS

Obviously, no discussion about customer service would be complete without the most important ingredient--the customer. It's strange, but true, that most organizations lose sight of their real purpose in life--to serve the customer. Certainly, numerous governmental organizations, civil servants, schools, parents, and, of course, businesses, have forgotten who butters their bread. Have you ever heard, or at least thought, "If it weren't for these damn customers, we could get something done?"

PRINCIPLES CONCERNING CUSTOMERS

Principle 1: The concept of managing "moments of truth" should be the primary driving philosophy of management.

Okay, so what's a "moment of truth?" Jan Carlzon, president of Scandinavian Airlines System, defines it as an episode in which a customer comes into contact with any aspect of the company, however remote, and thereby has an opportunity to form an impression. It could be an ad in the newspaper, the landscaping in front of your business, the way your receptionist answers your phone, your restrooms--anything with which a potential customer comes in contact.

Principle 2:

Rule #1--The customer is always right.

Rule #2--If the customer is wrong, see rule #1. Okay, so take this one with a grain of salt. Obviously, customers are sometimes wrong, even obnoxious. However, rather than winning the battle and losing the war, try minimizing the damage and attempt to building long-term relationships.

Principle 3: Treat customers like appreciating assets, like life-long partners. Be easy to do business with.

Principle 4: People buy only two things: GOOD FEELINGS and SOLUTIONS TO PROBLEMS. (One doesn't buy a quarter-inch drill; one buys a quarter-inch hole). Most psychologists agree we are generally in one of four modes: SCARED, SAD, MAD, or GLAD. Guess in which mode most people buy things?

Principle 5: How you think you are being perceived and how you are actually being perceived can be worlds apart. Customers aren't concerned with, nor do they care about, problems within your organization. (I can recall numerous instances where I have overheard employees arguing or complaining. I don't remember caring about their problems; I felt uncomfortable).

Principle 6: It's not the quality of service you give, but the quality of service the customer perceives that causes him or her to come back. PERCEIVED

SERVICE QUALITY is the difference between what they get and what they expect. Relative perceived quality is the single most important factor in determining long term profitability.

Principle 7: Make a customer checklist:

1. Don't guess what customers want (ask 'em)
2. Make it easy for them to tell you their opinions
3. Do it right the first time
4. Don't worry about being taken advantage of
5. Stay in touch
6. The answer is "yes"
7. One call should do it all
8. Educate the customer
9. Don't charge for extra service
10. "Good enough" never is

Principle 8: UNDER PROMISE--OVER DELIVER! (U.P.O.D.) How many times have you witnessed the reverse?

Principle 9: If something should go wrong:

A. Apologize
B. Fix the problem
C. Follow up

Principle 10: Your job and your organization exist because of, and for, the customer.

Do you get the impression nothing happens without customers? Then why do you suppose so many clerks, civil servants, politicians, colleges, parents, bureaucrats, and bankers act as if they are doing you a favor by waiting on you? It's up to each one of us to remind them that their very existence depends on us; WE ARE THEIR CUSTOMERS.

And, if you happen to be in one of their positions, take care of your customers.

HOW ARE WE DOING?

Okay, let's assume for a minute you have become convinced that excellent customer service is an absolute necessity, and you have instituted the necessary steps to implement it. How do you know how well your company is doing? You won't know, unless you ask.

So, how do you ask? Actually, numerous methods are available: on-site interviews, phone calls, survey cards, and suggestion boxes are just a few.

The real key to finding out what your customers think is to make it very easy for them to tell you. Have you ever heard the old saying, "No news is good news?" Not true. No news is definitely bad news.

Wouldn't it be nice, for example, if a waitperson asked you how the restaurant could better serve you instead of asking the customary, "Is everything okay?" I challenge you to ask customers questions which can't be answered "yes" or "no."

EMPLOYEES AND CO-WORKERS

"If you're not serving the customer, you'd better be serving someone who is." In my opinion, the most important aspect of customer service is the concept of providing excellent service to the "internal customer." In many cases, a company's internal customers are its employees.

The reason employees constitute such an important role in the success of a company's operation is because how customers feel about the people who serve them is a key factor in winning and keeping them. And yet, many times, employees and co-workers are overlooked, underpaid, overworked, and undertrained. Is it any wonder that the very people who have the most contact with the ultimate customer cause the relationship to fizzle?

What can management do?

1. Spend quality time with employees
2. Pay them well
3. Listen to them
4. Train them
5. Hire enough of them
6. Maintain a motivating environment
7. Recognize them

8. Hire effective people (it's easier to hire employees with good social skills, high self esteem, and tolerance for social contact than it is to motivate them to display those qualities)
9. Listen to them (they're the ones who make daily contact with customers)
10. EMPOWER THEM (give them the authority which coincides with their responsibilities)

The Eastern Missouri and Southern Illinois chapter of the Better Business Bureau, in its "Training Front-Line Employees" seminar, recommends teamwork. All employees and managers must work together to make sure the company's policy on customer service is put into practice. In most companies, an individual must depend on other people, other departments, and even suppliers to fulfill commitments to customers.

It goes on to say, "Effective teamwork depends upon the extent to which employees treat other employees as customers, feel that managers care about them, feel that they are cooperating rather than competing, and feel personally involved in and committed to customer satisfaction."

COMPANIES ENHANCING EMPLOYEES' EFFECTIVENESS

Southwest Airlines. Whenever the subject of excellent customers comes up, this company inevitably is mentioned. The company's CEO, Herbert Kelleher, is quoted in the August 29, 1992 issue of Fortune as saying, "Treating the customer right is a lot easier when employees are treating one another that way."

Each operating division at Southwest has identified its internal customer and focused on his or her needs. Mechanics who service planes target the pilots who fly them, and marketers do the same with reservations' agents. Thus, departments shower one another with free ice cream, pizza, or other goodies as tokens of customer devotion--or simply in appreciation of a job well done.

Employees who earn repeated commendations--sometimes called "Love Reports"--may earn perks: a free meal or a choice parking spot. Kelleher concludes: "The people who work here don't think of Southwest as a business. They think of it as a crusade."

United Services Automobile Association (USAA) This progressive company, whose headquarters are in San Antonio, has pioneered progressive employment practices like the four-day workweek, spends approximately $20 million on employee training, and is a leader in integrating minorities into its work force. The company's 286-acre headquarters' complex includes tennis courts, softball diamonds, jogging trails, artificial lakes, and 75 classrooms.

According to a company spokesperson, employees are empowered with knowledge. Millions of dollars are allocated annually for training and education, with over 200 full-time instructors and 75 classrooms. Before a service representative starts answering phones, he or she has received at least 16 weeks of training and job simulations.

USAA also has developed a tuition program. The company pays the fees for anybody studying for a business degree or taking a college course relevant to their job, provided they earn a C or better, or a B or better for graduate work.

Childress Buick, Phoenix. According to the October 1993 issue of The Service Edge, this car dealership made Inc. magazine's list of the small companies to work for in America. Rusty Childress says, "The prerequisite to external customer satisfaction and retention is employee satisfaction."

How does the company ensure employee satisfaction?

1. Rigorous orientation training. New employees spend one day a week for the first six weeks of their tenure working with a different department in the company.
2. Clear and consistent corporate communication. By utilizing a company newsletter and weekly electronic mail, the company promotes the idea that they are all

in a partnership working toward the same goals.

3. Strong focus on job autonomy. When employees feel their ideas will be listened to, they take a stronger sense of ownership in their jobs.

Northwest Airlines. Four months after Northwest Airlines narrowly avoided bankruptcy, the carrier's 44,000 unionized employees traded contract concessions for partial ownership of the company. The $886 million concession's deal included pay cuts of up to 15 percent in exchange for three of the 15 seats on the board of directors and an ownership stake of up to 37.5 percent.

Says one of the pilots, "If Northwest is successful, employees will share in it. If it's not, they're one of the reasons."

KCN Company Builders. This company is a small custom-home building company which utilizes subcontractors to do its work. However, most of the subcontractors have been working for the company for 15 to 20 years and many feel as if they are part of the company. To cement that relationship, the company recently initiated its annual "Shooting Star Customer Service Award."

Based on customer surveys, as well as on personal observations, recipients are awarded a $100 stipend, a certificate for framing, and recognition in local newspapers. The idea quickly caught on and now the subcontractors are redoubling their efforts to win the coveted award.

The five foregoing examples are but of the few which we could discuss, but I think you get the picture: YOUR EMPLOYEES ARE THE KEY TO OBTAINING AND RETAINING CUSTOMERS.

WHAT CAN YOU, THE EMPLOYEE, DO? DEVELOP A NEW MIND-SET.

1. The most important goal of any employee, including salespeople, should be to create and keep customers.

2. You are the greatest customer you'll ever win. Your world is a mirror and your mind is a magnet. What you perceive in this world is largely a reflection of your attitudes and beliefs.

3. Develop a genuine interest in your customers. Establish rapport; let them know that you're thinking about them.

4. Try to understand the frustrations your customers face; try to see things from the customer's point of view.

5. Your job, and your organization, exist because of and for the customer. As I stated earlier, it is easier to hire motivated people than to motivate people. Even though some consider me as a motivational speaker, I frankly doubt that I can

motivate anyone--especially if they don't want to be motivated.

Oh, I'm sure that a stirring motivational talk will have a temporary effect, but I doubt that it will have a lasting effect. On the other hand, employers can create a motivational atmosphere, a learning environment, and a friendly arena in which to work.

By the same token, employees can ensure their success by becoming well-rounded persons.

THE ROAD OF LIFE

I believe that the "better-rounded" a person becomes the more effective that person will be as an employee--thereby making that person more effective with customers.

What a difference a few years makes. I remember as a business graduate student we learned that the key to successful management was to con employees into making their goals and the company's goals the same. As our society has progressed, however, we find that workaholics are not necessarily the company pillars they once were thought to be (Sometimes they even become "burned out" and do stupid things).

Now, before you business owners and managers write me nasty letters, consider this: doesn't it make sense that employees become more effective as their education, community involvement, professional development, and family relationships improve? Oh, it may be true that, in the short term, total dedication to the job may appear to be the optimum situation, but in the long term, well-rounded employees will increasingly contribute as their self esteem grows.

I have arbitrarily selected eight major areas in which I believe it is important to become involved:

1. Social adeptness
2. Spiritual growth
3. Physical maintenance
4. Family relationships
5. Financial security
6. Professional development
7. Civic involvement
8. Mental enhancement

SELF-TEST

Below are some questions you might want to ask yourself to determine how you rate in each of the aforementioned categories.

SOCIAL ADEPTNESS (Rate yourself on each, 1 to 10)

Do you have a variety of close friends? _____
Do you develop friendships readily? _____
Do you enjoy meeting new people, going to parties, etc.? _____

Total _____

SPIRITUAL GROWTH (Rate yourself on each, 1 to 10)

Do you spend time alone to think, meditate, pray? _____

Have you studied the Bible or religious history? _____

Do you regularly attend a church or a synagogue? _____

Total _____

PHYSICAL MAINTENANCE (Rate yourself on each, 1 to 10)

Do you exercise regularly? _____

Do you eat nutritious, well-balanced meals? _____

Are you involved in playing sports? _____

Total _____

FAMILY RELATIONSHIPS (Rate yourself on each, 1 to 10)

Do you spend quality and quantity time with your family? _____

Do you regularly write or call your family? _____

Do you enjoy family reunions or gatherings? _____

Total _____

FINANCIAL SECURITY (Rate yourself on each, 1 to 10)

Do you have a job that pays well? _____

Are you creating a secure retirement fund? _____

Do you have substantial investments? _____

Total _____

PROFESSIONAL DEVELOPMENT (Rate yourself on each, 1 to 10)

Are you fulfilled by your career? _____

Are there opportunities for advancement? _____

Are you good at what you do? Do you enjoy it? _____

Total _____

CIVIC INVOLVEMENT (Rate yourself on each, 1 to 10)

Are you involved in community or civic activities? _____

Do you belong to community or civic associations? _____

Have you volunteered for community or civic projects? _____

Total _____

MENTAL ENHANCEMENT (Rate yourself on each, 1 to 10)

Do you enjoy reading nonfiction books? _____

Do you enjoy educational TV programs? _____

Do you like museums, fairs, libraries, etc.?_____

Total _____

Now plot your score along the bar graph and connect the dots to see how straight your path is. Are there a few kinks which you can take out? Are there a few areas that require some attention?

THE ROAD OF LIFE

	1	5	10	15	20	25	30
Social Adeptness							
Spiritual Growth							
Physical Maintenance							
Family Relations							
Financial Security							
Professional Development							
Civic Involvement							
Mental Enhancement							

I believe that the straighter and farther to the right your path is, the more effective a person you will be, both in your professional life and in your personal life.

TQM (TOTAL QUALITY MANAGEMENT)

Whoa! Another term! Just exactly what <u>is</u> TQM? How does it work? What good is it? How will it help your life and your company's bottom line?

Total Quality Management (TQM) is basically a customer-driven, quality-obsessed business approach. Its focus is on the customer and on quality as it is perceived by the customer.

Stephen Chopart, editor-in-chief of Business Week magazine, states, "Quality may be the biggest competitive issue of the late 20th and 21st centuries." Companies and service organizations are discovering that quality is as vital a marketing tool as price.

As one reviews the TQM concept, three gurus' names keep popping up--Deming, Crosby, and Juran. All have contributed a substantial amount, and all disagree on various points.

Philip B. Crosby's fame rests primarily upon his "zero defects" concept. It means that management receives what it asks for, and that if it wants a certain percentage of nonconforming material, then it will receive that percentage. In other words, "zero defects" is another way of saying "do it right the first time."

Crosby says, "Quality management is a systematic way of guaranteeing that organized activities happen the way they are planned. It is a management discipline concerned with preventing problems from occurring by creating the attitudes and controls that make prevention possible."

Although Joseph Juran, the second TQM guru, followed Deming to Japan, he is given much credit by the Japanese for elevating quality control to a management tool. In fact, some believe Deming borrowed many of his ideas from Juran. His detractors say that while Deming is a visionary, Juran is a pragmatist--advocating a "nuts and bolts" approach to quality management.

The major leader in the TQM movement is unquestionably W. Edwards Deming. He is critical of Crosby's "zero defects" philosophy because, in his opinion, it confuses the crucial difference between product quality and process quality. He believes that companies would do better by focusing on constant improvement rather than by focusing on the impossible goal of zero defects.

Deming, who initially developed the total quality management concept in Japan, believes that "a satisfied customer is not enough." He stresses that business is built on loyal customers, who keep on coming back--and who bring friends with them.

His message consistently stresses the needs of customers. He believes that quality products, quality processes, and quality management are all necessary to ensure customer satisfaction. In fact, he believes that quality and customers should always be placed ahead of company profits. (The fact is, if the first three items are successfully achieved, company profits will automatically follow).

Deming is known for his Fourteen Points, management's commandments for formulating key quality management's practices. I won't use the space in this book to list and explain them, but let me quickly summarize the principles which apply:

1. Quality is defined by the customer.
2. Reducing variation in every process is a must.

3. Top management must be committed to improvement.
4. Change and improvement must include everyone--including outside suppliers.
5. There must be ongoing education and training for all employees.
6. Eliminate individual employee rating's systems.

So, there you have it--a quick synopsis of the three leading TQM advocates. There are numerous books that you can read to help you further understand each one's philosophies. It is my purpose only to introduce you to TQM's concepts and to wet your appetite to learn more about them.

TQM SHORTCOMINGS

Not everyone, however, is excited about the concept of Total Quality Management, at least as it is defined by the gurus which we have discussed. Why?

According to TARP, quality is getting a bad name due to poor results. Frequently, there is operational impact but little additional value to the customer.

To explain further, despite rhetoric to the contrary, quality improvement priorities are often not customer driven. In other words, priorities are set based on management's perception of key customer problems. Unfortunately, their perceptions are frequently wrong. Second, the results of TQM efforts often are not tracked in a manner which allows what works in the marketplace to be separated from what does not work.

In my opinion, it is tempting, at least when following Deming's precepts, to get hung up on procedures rather than on results. And, after all, it's results that really matter.

While it's true that simply smiling at customers is not the complete answer to providing excellent customer service, neither is the obsession with developing customer-oriented attitudes and customer-friendly procedures. So let's coin a new term: TCF (Total Customer Focus).

WE CAN'T BE HUMAN ALONE

Emperor Frederick, 13th century ruler of the Holy Roman Empire, wanted to determine what language Adam and Eve spoke in the Garden of Eden. His theory was that if babies could be isolated and never spoken to, they would, at the right time, begin speaking God's "original language."

So, he permanently "borrowed" a group of newborn babies, placed them in an area he thought resembled the Garden of Eden, and awaited the results. Wet nurses attended to the babies' every physical need, but they were forbidden to speak to each other or to the infants.

All the babies died.

The point is this: we can't be human alone. We must communicate with each other. Eighty percent of those who fail at work do so because they don't relate well to others.

In a study of 10,000 "de-hires," the Carnegie Institute of Technology ascertained that 95% were let go because of their inability to communicate with others.

Four hundred fifty-seven (457) members of the Academy of Certified Administrative Managers ranked 20 traits or competencies in order of importance. Two of the top four involved some form of communications.

So, what's the point? Just this: The better you learn to communicate with others, the better you will be able to serve them. Where can you start?------By listening!

LISTENING TO LEARN

I sincerely believe too many of us plan what we will say while the other person is still talking, rather than listening to what that person is saying. I mean, really listening.

How many times have you told someone something and she responds with, "Yeah, I hear you." And that's probably exactly what she means: She heard you, but she wasn't really listening.

What's the difference between hearing and listening? Well, hearing is merely a physical occurrence whereby sounds are registered in a person's ear. It requires no effort. On the other hand, listening is hearing with a purpose. It requires attention, thought, and concentration. It focuses not only on what is being said, but also on how it is being said.

BENEFITS OF LISTENING

As I mentioned at the outset, this book takes a holistic approach on the subject of customer service. I happen to believe that the more well-rounded a person becomes, the better that person will be able (and willing) to serve fellow human beings. And since poor listening habits seem to permeate the very fabric of our society, it is necessary to be made aware that this phenomenon exists and is detrimental to our overall well-being. It is also necessary to learn how to counteract this phenomenon.

What are some of the benefits of becoming a good listener?

1. Improved personal relationships
2. More professional image
3. Better resolution of conflicts
4. Ability to better absorb information
5. Improved negotiating abilities
6. Improved self esteem
7. Diffuses tense situations
8. Makes selling easier
9. Listening is persuasive
10. Helps develop and maintain rapport

Can you see how these benefits might help you become better at serving fellow human beings? Can you see how these benefits might help you toward success?

OBSTACLES TO EFFECTIVE LISTENING

Okay, let's assume for a minute that you buy into the benefits of listening. Why, then, is it so difficult to really listen? Listed below are some obstacles encountered in trying to listen.

1. Negative feelings about the speaker--clothes you don't like, poor posture, or bad grooming. (Admit it--it's more difficult to listen to one who doesn't look "like he or she should").

2. Bias toward the speaker's subject--For instance, it would be difficult for anyone to persuade me that communism is a great political and social system, no matter how good a speaker he or she may be.

3. Undesirable voice--Let's be honest. It's difficult to listen to someone with a squeaky, raspy, timid, bellowing, and/or monotone voice.

4. Poor eye contact--Remember when you were a kid? Didn't your mother tell you to look her in

the eye? We still want people to look us in the eye. Someone with shifty eyes simply looks insincere, or even dishonest.

5. Invading your space--Are you familiar with the 36-24-12 rule? Simply stated, it means that new acquaintances, business colleagues, etc., generally feel comfortable speaking to each other at a distance of about 36 inches. Casual friends generally feel comfortable at about 24 inches. Intimate friends and lovers generally feel comfortable at about 12 inches (or less). Remember that so that you don't invade someone's "space."

Also keep that in mind before you throw your briefcase onto someone's desk or sit too closely to them during a presentation or interview.

How do you know if you are too close? He may mask his face with his hands or with paper. Her eyes may blink too frequently. He may hunch, rock, turn, look away, drum his fingers, or move or lean away to re-establish a comfortable distance.

6. Physical environment--It's difficult to talk over the noise of machinery, traffic, or other voices. (Also, something you might want to remember when your kids or your spouse need to talk with you--turn off the TV). In other words, if you have

control of the situation, make the atmosphere conducive to listening.

7. Condition of the listener--What if you're too tired or stressed to listen? I remember when our daughters were young and they wanted to play the minute I walked through the door after work. My wife usually arranged for me to have a few minutes of quiet and time alone before she allowed the onslaught to begin.

How many obstacles can you envision? It's better to think of them in advance so you can plan around them better. After all, effective listening is one of the most important functions you must perform in order to enhance excellence in customer service.

The average person listens at an effective rate of only 25%. An individual's immediate recall on the average is only 50%, and within 48 hours it drops to 25%. On the phone, it's even worse.

Another reason we are such poor listeners is that we can listen to, and comprehend, 600 to 900 words per minute; yet most people speak from 125 to 180 words per minute. So, our minds become bored and substitute something else to think about instead of to what we're supposed to be listening.

IMPROVING OUR LISTENING SKILLS

Are you still with me? Do you agree that the level of listening skills you possess can make a vast difference in your effectiveness in the customer service arena? If you don't, then start over at the beginning of this chapter and answer the question again. If you <u>do</u> agree, then continue.

Now that we know <u>why</u>, let's review <u>how</u> we can improve our listening skills.

1. <u>Listen for the total meaning.</u> Listen for <u>what</u> is being said, what is <u>not</u> being said, and for what the speaker would <u>like</u> to say but cannot put into words. Real estate agents, for instance, commonly encounter clients who say something like, "Nothing is too good for my family." While we certainly agree with the client, we frequently find that what he really means is that "nothing is too good for his family as long as he can afford what his family wants."

2. <u>Force yourself to wait before you answer or react.</u> Parents, especially, must remain aware of the temptation to "fly off the handle" before their child has a chance to finish telling them what went wrong at school that day. It's especially important to wait if you want your child to continue to share her experiences with you.

3. Stop talking. I believe many sales people talk themselves into, and then right out of, sales. People love to hear themselves talk, so let the other person become impressed with you by allowing her to talk. This is especially important when a customer has a complaint. Let her get it off her chest. She will usually turn from a lion into a lamb.

4. Don't jump to conclusions. This one is closely related to the previous two aspects. We've "heard it all," right? So we already know what is about to be said, right? In many cases, no.

I had a personal experience several years ago which reiterated the need to shut up, to listen, and not jump to conclusions. I was flying to the Texas' Rio Grande Valley to deliver a speech and was sitting next to a gentleman from Missouri. He and his wife had been attending a Farm Bureau convention in San Antonio and were headed to Mexico to go shopping.

Anyway, he began telling me a story I thought would never end. Have you ever had that experience? He was the slowest speaker I had ever witnessed and it was all I could do to remain interested in what he was saying. He had trouble finding the words to finish a particular sentence and I was sorely tempted to finish it for him. Fortunately, I didn't, and it was a good thing because it ended completely different than I expected. Fortunately, it was a relatively short flight.

5. Watch body language. There are numerous books covering the subject of body language, so I am not going to pursue any details in this book. However, there are tell-tale signs you must be able to recognize in order to become a better listener.

Some simple ones to watch for are listed below.

1. More than two nods of the head indicates insincerity
2. Looking suddenly up and to the side indicates skepticism
3. An "open" position (arms and legs) indicates an open attitude
4. Hands on hips indicate anger
5. Feet pointed toward the door indicates a mental departure
6. Ask questions. This one should have a double star beside it because it's the most important one.

The person who asks the questions controls the conversation. If only we could persuade the fast-talking salesperson.

Relationships are in; "one-night stands" are out. It's true in our personal, social, and spiritual worlds as well as in the business world. The more high tech we become, the more high touch is desired. Everyone wants to be a person; nobody wants to be a number.

How do we achieve high touch? By asking questions--open ended questions which cannot be answered with a "yes" or "no"--lots of questions. Find out what the other person's hot button is. Find out what makes him tick. Find out what turns her on and what turns her off. Find out how you can better serve him. (Wouldn't it be nice, for instance, if the waiter, instead of uttering an inane, "Is everything OK?" would ask, "What can we do to better serve you?"

Find out what you are doing wrong, what you are doing right, and what your competitors are doing right or wrong. Make it easy for someone to tell you what you want to know. No news is not necessarily good news. (As I mentioned in a previous chapter, most dissatisfied customers will not bother to tell you).

Ask questions, and then stop talking so you can listen to the answers. Many of us have been trained how to speak, how to perform, and how to present. But most of us have never been trained how to listen. So it's up to you to train yourself. It's not easy. It takes patience and practice. But it is achievable and it will pay huge dividends.

5

LIP SERVICE OR CUSTOMER SERVICE?

In an extensive American Management Association survey, respondents see service to the customer as more or as much more important to their businesses in the future. Almost 78 percent agree that improving customer service and quality are the key to competitive success.

However, the survey reports, there exists a vast gap between the kind of service companies want to give and their actual performance. This phenomenon was most certainly confirmed by the survey we conducted.

This chapter will illustrate the “state of customer service” as it currently exists. Various types of companies and industries will be discussed in a casual, reader-friendly way so that you will be able to understand exactly what is going on in a general way in the customer service arena. Then, Chapters 7 and 8 will get more specific as we reveal the results of our own survey.

MOST SERVICE CONSIDERED MEDIOCRE

Do you consider yourself to be a better-than-average driver? Doesn't everyone? Yet, the truth is, many of us are poor to mediocre drivers.

The same is true of customer service. Almost every company and organization believe they exhibit better-than-average customer service. The truth is, most of us would probably agree that customer service in this country is, at best, mediocre.

Airlines can't get you (or your luggage) there on time; fix-it shops can't fix it; bankers are too important to talk to you; hospitals work patients over and make them sicker; schools treat their teachers and students like criminals and, restaurants run diners through like a herd of cattle. We, the public, are not happy campers.

TQM

TQM's adherents preach that factors other than excellence in service are what really count. They say a product's price/performance, quality ratings as determined by the industry, and the specifications of the product relative to the purchaser's requirements constitute the real elements of true customer service.

True customer service, however, says "the product is what the product does." It is the total package of benefits customers receive when they buy it - functional utility, technical assistance, training, and repair services after the sale.

TOTAL CUSTOMER FOCUS (TCF)

The race to please customers has just begun. In fact, according to David Altany in Industry Week, competition is heating up to the point that companies are finding that "just" satisfying customers is only an intermediate goal, a prerequisite to staying in business. To prosper, and to differentiate themselves from competitors, companies are discovering that they must reach beyond customer satisfaction.

While I am not advocating that you should ignore the principles of TQM, the process of adding more value to products should be thought out carefully before taking the plunge. Costly improvements for things the customers don't really want add little or no value to a product or service.

Again, according to Altany, by far the most inexpensive way to add value to products or services is to apply the personal touch to routine encounters and procedures. Customers are more impressed by friendly, personalized contact than by any other service factors--including speedy delivery, defect-free products, and convenience.

WON'T PAY FOR SERVICE

Despite what I have just said about personalized service outdistancing technical aspects of a product or service, customers are willing to pay for quality, but they are not willing to pay for excellent service. Furthermore, the more a company tries to get customers to pay for service, the more resistance there will be.

According to Edward de Bono, in the November 1990 issue of Business Marketing, "There are some values that may be expensive to provide and that may be very much appreciated. But buyers refuse to pay for them. Attempts to charge for these values or to insert them too obviously into the overall price leads to customer resistance. Conversely, including these values at no extra charge gives a product or service considerable advantage."

In other words, warmth and charm are expected. They are taken for granted, like oil in a machine. The money involved in providing excellent service and flexibility can no longer be considered as a cost. It has to be considered as product quality.

A recent poll revealed that an overwhelming majority (over 81 percent) agree that focusing on the customer is the single biggest competitive advantage. It was by far more important than price or product performance. Customer focus is, in fact, the single thread which binds the rest together.

HOW ARE YOU DOING? AND HOW DO YOU FIND OUT?

Ultimately, the only thing which matters is how you and your product/service are being perceived by the customer. All of the rest--industry awards, achievement of production goals, beating the industry benchmark--are of little value if your customers don't like what you're doing.

A good example of what I'm referring to occurs within the entertainment industry. Participants are forever patting themselves on the back (the Oscars, the Grammy's, the Tony's), but in many cases, forgetting all about their customers.

Okay, let's assume you agree. How are you doing and how do you find out? After all, no one wants to listen to customer complaints, right? Whoa!

A sure sign of a bad or a worsening relationship is the absence of customer complaints. Yeah, I know it's always nice to hear compliments, but it's more important to hear it all--the good and the bad. Remember? The customer who has his complaint taken seriously will be more loyal than before. How do you find out? Ask.

Almost every store, hotel, restaurant, and even the post office have survey cards for you to fill out. You can do the same thing.

ONE WHICH HAS EXCELLED

In an industry where competitors are barely distinguishable from one another, in an age where air transport is just another commodity, one airline stands out from all the rest. For the past few years, headlines about this company read as follows:

- "Southwest Airlines - Where Service Flies Right"
- "Southwest Airlines Ranked Tops in Quality Study"
- "Southwest Number 1 in Quality Survey"
- "Taking Off - Southwest Airlines a Texas Maverick"
- "Southwest Ranks Number 1 Based on Market Value"

What a coincidence! Isn't it amazing that the airline company which excels in "dignifying the customer" also enjoys the largest market value of all publicly held U.S. airlines? Isn't it amazing that the airline company which ranks first in quality service also swims in a sea of job applications? Isn't it amazing that the airline company which personally answers customer's letters also is one of the few profitable airlines in existence today?

I didn't bother to survey Southwest Airlines because I already knew the answers I would get. Yes, they are committed to customer service. Yes, they regularly try to exceed customer expectations. Yes, the quality of their service is measured by their customers. Yes, they treat their employees as they expect their employees to treat their customers. Yes, employees are expected to do what it takes to meet or exceed customer expectations.

So, you see, there was no need to interview them. They are a beacon, not only to their industry, but to business in general.

SOME WHICH HAVEN'T

Consumers unhappy about purchases of products or services registered 1,480,777 complaints with Better Business Bureau offices across the country in 1993. Remember, however, that for every complaint registered to the BBB, there are probably hundreds of complaints that were simply delivered verbally. Also, remember that for every complaint aired, there are 9 others which aren't. Finally, remember that unhappy customers will tell an average of 10 others about their negative experience.

But, just for kicks, lets assume that all complaints during 1993 were aired with the BBB -

1,480,777. Now, let's assume that for each complaint aired, there were 9 additional which weren't (1,480,777 x 9 = 13,326,993!). Of course, as I said earlier, there are millions of complaints which are never registered with the BBB, so the real total of complaints is almost incalculable.

WHAT DOES IT ALL MEAN?

I believe that the creation and distribution of goods and services enhances our lives. I also believe that an obsession with excellent customer service makes it more pleasant and profitable for everyone concerned.

Too many businesses in this country have, instead, become obsessed with the bottom line. If there were only one thing for which I could convince those businesses, it is this: Focus on serving your fellow human beings-- customers, employees, neighbors, friends, and children. It will bring you great personal rewards and robust bottom lines.

Life is not lost by dying; it is lost by not caring. Life is dignified through serving, not by being served. When you focus on serving, your work is no longer just a trade-out for money; you dignify your existence.

KCN COMPANIES

While I was still in the United States Navy, I had a dream, a burning desire, to create a tourist attraction that would portray the State of Texas as it existed in the 1870's. I thought about it constantly and became obsessed with the idea.

After I was discharged from the Navy, I began putting my plans into action. I was able to convince the marketing department at the University of Texas Graduate School of Business to conduct a marketing survey/feasibility study for me. I was able to convince an artist to construct models. In addition, I was able to delude myself into believing the project would really work.

I believed it so much that I obtained an option on several hundreds of acres of land north of San Antonio on which to build my dream. It's ironic, isn't it, that the future would find me advocating such things as dreaming, planning, goal-setting, etc. What I was to learn in the future, however, was that dreams and plans and goal-setting must be based upon some sort of reality. Then, they become real dreams, not just pipe dreams.

Anyway, it became obvious even to me after a year of chasing possible investors that the project was doomed. I tried to exist without an income, my wife delivered our first-born daughter, and I was not being a responsible "bread-winner." And, my self-esteem was suffering immensely.

SAVING GRACE

Sometimes, things have a uncanny way of working out for the best. My "Texas" project was obviously doomed to failure, but I still held an option on that piece of ranch land. So, my father-in-law and a stockholder in a home-building company, Mr. Fred Reeb, suggested that I contact the president of the home-building company to ascertain if he might be interested in the property for development purposes.

It just so happened that he was interested, and it also just so happened that he needed an assistant to help develop the property. (Enter yours truly).

The rest is predictable history. I went to work for the building company, learned the ropes, so to speak, and branched out on my own five years later - enter KCN Company.

The year was 1976 - January 1, to be exact. I embarked on a new life; I was full of anticipation, full of anxiety, and full of fear. The previous 5 years had been invaluable. I had learned quite a bit about the building business and quite a bit about how to deal with fellow human beings. I had also learned a lot about what not to do. Now the ball was in my court.

Success came quickly. We began making money almost immediately and I began wondering why I had waited so long to "make the break." I found out in later years that the economy wouldn't always be so kind to me.

EARLY CUSTOMER SERVICE

You know, it's easy to practice excellent customer service when one is scared to death that the business might fail. It's easy to practice excellent customer service when one is new in the business. It's easy to practice excellent customer service when one isn't so busy. But the key is, can you still exhibit excellent customer service when you are really established, confident, and busy?

You've probably heard the old adage, "If it weren't for all those damn customers I could get something done." Wow! What an attitude. Unfortunately, that kind of attitude seems to permeate American business today.

Oh, to be sure, it's fashionable and politically correct to tout customer service as the cornerstone of a business, but unfortunately most organizations pay only lip service rather than real customer service. It's not easy to provide really excellent customer service, especially when things are going well and the company is making a lot of money.

Anyway, at first it was easy to practice excellent customer service because I realized how important it was to attract new customers - especially since I didn't have many. For the first year or so after I began my own building business, my wife and I worked seven days a week, building houses, cleaning houses, and selling houses.

We followed up on every telephone call, distributed flyers and leaflets, and attended every meeting and social event possible in order to "stay in front of people." It was imperative that we establish name recognition and credibility as quickly as possible.

I personally supervised every construction project and paid special attention to every detail. My company quickly became recognized as the premier home building firm in our area. As a matter of fact, demand for our services grew so rapidly that it became apparent to me that I could not begin to keep up with the demand. Consequently, I began looking for a field superintendent to help me supervise jobs.

SPIRALING DOWNWARD

From 1978 to 1986 (eight years), I employed field superintendents to assist me. At first it seemed to be the right thing to do because it really relieved me of having to take care of so many little details. I relaxed more and enjoyed my new-found "executive lifestyle."

Okay, so it was costing my company a substantial amount of money to support a superintendent, but after all, it would be worth it in the future, right? Theoretically, we could build enough extra homes to make up for the extra cost. Furthermore, I could enjoy myself more and live longer.

The fact that we were receiving more and more customer complaints really didn't affect me at first. And the fact that my subcontractors were unhappy wasn't really a problem either -- or so I thought. But the fact that our business began decreasing caught my attention.

NEW-FOUND PURPOSE

I underwent an "attitude adjustment" at about the same time that my income stopped. Funny how that happens, isn't it? It's simply amazing how quickly one can become humble when things aren't going too well.

The Texas economy was bleak during the 1986-1989 era and we existed on almost no income at all. My wife, who had been out of the classroom for 19 years, subsequently returned to teaching and attended graduate school. Those were tough times and I became a fairly good "house husband."

I fully supported her efforts. I mean, at least one of us had to have a steady income and it certainly wasn't coming from me. Those were depressing times, but those lean years taught us some valuable lessons.

The most important lesson I learned as a result of the tough years was that if my company was to get on its feet again, <u>customer service would have to become top priority</u>.

BACK ON OUR FEET AGAIN

As a result of my negative experiences during the downturn in the economy, I decided to take the bull by the horns and institute a program consisting of innovative ideas and of unparalleled customer service.

First, after I had conducted a substantial amount of market research and determined a need for a new kind of service, I launched a new division that specialized in building small, inexpensive cedar custom homes. I called the division "Ranch Houses of the West." Never have I witnessed such great amount of interest from the public.

Finally, those on limited incomes, young couples, and retirees had access to having a custom home built on their property at a reasonable cost. We continued, of course, to offer our regular estate-type custom homes, but at the time there wasn't much demand for those. Our Ranch House business took off like a rocket.

SHOOTING STAR AWARD

Simultaneously, I inaugurated a new program called "Shooting Star Customer Service Excellence." We sent surveys to customers whose homes we had recently completed and asked them to rate everyone involved with our company - including me as the builder.

Based upon the surveys and upon the support subcontractors gave me, I began awarding a personalized certificate (and a $100 stipend to the winning contractors) and submitted their pictures to the local newspapers.

The first year, two subcontractors were recognized. I'm sure that the $100 disappeared quickly, but I've seen their certificates on their walls.

Almost immediately, other subcontractors began calling my assistant to find out how they also could become winners. The second year saw five subcontractors recognized.

So what's the purpose of the Shooting Star Award? Even though I have always realized that as a builder I am only as good or as bad as the contractors make me appear, I decided that I really wanted to make them part of my team. After all, we are all in this together, just as we are in all of life.

I felt that it was high time to "put my money where my mouth was." I had always admitted the importance of having loyal subcontractors, but I decided that I needed to establish a highly visible program which would simultaneously give the winners the credit they deserved and position my company yet another step ahead of the competition.

It worked, and it is still working. I sincerely hope the day will come when all of my contractors qualify for the Shooting Star Award.

DIFFICULTIES

As is the case with any programs, new or old, there are some negative aspects. For instance, after I had awarded the first year's Shooting Star Awards, a couple of my other subcontractors complained that they had been overlooked even though, in their opinion, they had deserved to win. Well, we don't always agree with the referee at a football game either, but it's still his call, isn't it?

I felt badly about having to leave some of the contractors out, but in order for the award to have any real meaning, it had to be tough to win. If I had awarded everyone, I would have not only failed to make my point, but I would have wasted money, too. Fortunately, one of the contractors who complained about not winning the first year was a winner the second year. (The other one quit).

Overall, however, I think that the Shooting Star Award program can be deemed a huge success. As I am writing this book, I am contemplating a program whereby I can make my suppliers a part of my company also.

TOO BUSY

As I stated earlier, a home builder is dependent upon numerous other people - contractors, suppliers, lenders, and Realtors - just to name a few. The greatest challenge in the home building business is to coordinate the activities of all the various entities and make them all connect in a meaningful manner at the end.

Theoretically, the process should be simple: order necessary materials, schedule the appropriate contractors at the appropriate times, and close out the house on time. Sounds easy, doesn't it? Well, it would be if only everyone did everything that should be done, when it should be done, and how it should be done. The problem is, of course, that in real life things just don't work out like they are supposed to.

Materials don't arrive on time; some of their parts are missing; contractors don't finish their previous jobs; and, consequently, begin yours late. Their memories lapse just when they should be their sharpest.

Now all of this wouldn't be so bad, except for the customer. He or she simply doesn't understand the problem. All the customer cares about is being able to move into the new home on time and having a minimum of problems arise. (Any builder will tell you that "go-backs" are the most hated part of the building business. Customers simply don't understand why there should even be "go-backs").

Ironically, the most difficult part of my business occurs during the "good" times. I remember only a few years ago when business was almost nonexistent, suppliers and contractors were ready, willing, and able and jumped at my beckoned call.

Everyone was so grateful to be able to work they were extremely helpful. Customer service on their part was excellent, and consequently, excellent customer service on my part was easy to maintain, too. Sometimes I wish that business would slow down just a bit so we could all catch our collective breaths.

Because of the high demand for products and services now, though, everyone seems to running around trying to do everything for everybody. Consequently, nobody is doing a very good job for anybody.

Excellence in customer service is much more difficult to maintain during boom business times. However, I believe that it is vital to maintain a high level of service even during these times in order to build a base from which to operate later.

It's rather similar to the advertising concept. The time to advertise is when business is good. Most businesses seem to think that advertising isn't necessary during good times so they ignore it. Then, when business slows down, they begin advertising in earnest. I believe that businesses should become a familiar sound and sight during good times so that the public will remember them during slow times.

And what's one of the best forms of advertising and marketing? Excellent customer service! So do it, especially when you don't have to. It will pay huge dividends in the future.

AND AIM FOR EXCELLENCE

7

NATIONWIDE SURVEY

For the past several years I have been conducting customer service seminars entitled "Don't Shoot the Customer"--the same as this book. The information I have been sharing with my audiences generally came from my readings and from my personal business experiences, primarily in the custom home-building business.

As time went on, however, it became apparent to me that although my information had been gathered from reliable sources, it was necessary that I conduct my own research. By doing so, I would either collaborate or refute previous findings.

By utilizing bits and pieces from other researchers' surveys, as well as from several customer service managers who graciously shared their time and expertise with me, I devised a simple survey questionnaire. Along with a cover letter, I sent the survey to high-ranking officers of corporations and associations across the country. Most were consumer affairs managers, vice-presidents, and CEO's.

My staff mailed 680 survey questionnaires and received 72 responses--over 10%--67 signed and 5 anonymous. The 67 participants who took the time to complete the questionnaire, and who were brave enough to sign their names, are listed in Appendix 1

Figure 7-A

CUSTOMER SERVICE QUESTIONNAIRE

Please rate the following statements as they describe your organization. Please circle the most appropriate answer.

		Not at all	A little	Some-what	Quite a bit	Describes it exactly
1.	Our organization is <u>totally</u> committed to providing excellent customer service.	1	2	3	4	5
2.	Our goal is to regularly <u>exceed</u> customer expectations.	1	2	3	4	5
3.	The quality of our product or services is measured by our customers.	1	2	3	4	5
4.	Quality is defined as a "conformance to requirements."	1	2	3	4	5
5.	Our employees are expected to follow procedures in all customer service situations.	1	2	3	4	5
6.	We treat our employees as we expect them to treat our customers.	1	2	3	4	5
7.	We regularly request feedback from our customers.	1	2	3	4	5
8.	We utilized information from our customers to design our products and services.	1	2	3	4	5
9.	We make it easy for customers to complain to us.	1	2	3	4	5

10.	We educate our customers to most effectively utilize our products and services.	1	2	3	4
11.	A part of each executive's job is direct customer contact.	1	2	3	4
12.	Our employees at various levels meet directly with customers.	1	2	3	4
13.	All employees are expected to do what it takes to meet or exceed customer expectations.	1	2	3	4
14.	Employees are recognized and/or rewarded for "bending the rules" to meet a customer's need.	1	2	3	4
15.	All employees are routinely educated about our products and services.	1	2	3	4
16.	All levels of employees have a say in how their job is performed and measured.	1	2	3	4
17.	Our employees are cross-trained so that they fill in for each other.	1	2	3	4
18.	Employees do what it takes to help a customer even if it "isn't their job."	1	2	3	4
19.	The first criteria for promotion is customer service, whether internal or external customers.	1	2	3	4
20.	Continuing self development, college, or professional designation courses are encouraged.	1	2	3	4
21.	Self development is supported with financial aid.	1	2	3	4
22.	Self development must be outside of normal work hours.	1	2	3	4

23.	Departmental boundaries are intentionally invisible to the customer.	1	2	3	4
24.	Teamwork is rewarded above individual accomplishment.	1	2	3	4
25.	Our organization department heads work together to eliminate mistakes and defects before they occur.	1	2	3	4

* * * * * * * *

Please answer the following to the best of your ability:

1. Who are your internal customers?

2. Who are your external customers?

* * * * * * * *

What is your organization's mission statement? (Or enclose copy.)

* * * * * * * *

Specifically, what is (are) the greatest problem(s) your organization faces today?

* * * * * * * *

If you have a favorite customer service success story for your company please describe it.

See Figure 7-A for a copy of the questionnaire we mailed out. As you can see, we asked each participant to rate his/her organization on each of the 25 statements. Then, we asked each participant to answer several additional questions:

1. Who are your internal customers?
2. Who are your external customers?

We requested a copy of each organization's mission statement, a summary of each organization's greatest problems, and a narrative of a favorite customer service success story.

Most of the participants knew who their internal and external customers were, several included their mission statements and shared problems facing their organizations, but disturbingly few included customer service success stories.

After receiving the surveys, I spoke by phone or in person with several of the participants. I will share some of those conversations with you in the next chapter.

GENERAL FINDINGS

First of all, I suppose that a return of over 10% should be considered quite good, considering that usually only 3% of mail requests are returned. However, when one considers the fact that we were dealing with customer service-oriented people such as service managers, vice-presidents, and CEO's, it is rather disappointing to realize that almost 90% did not return the surveys.

One has to wonder what type of customer service these organizations harbor. If top executives are not proud enough to share their programs with the public, one wonders if they also aren't proud enough to share them with their customers. Or worse yet, maybe they don't have a viable customer service program.

I mean, the executives we targeted are supposedly the "creme de la creme" of the service world. We did receive several well-written letters explaining how it would be too time-consuming to complete the survey, but that they, nevertheless, appreciated the opportunity to do so. Ironically, the survey could have been completed in less time than it took to initiate and execute the letters.

ALARMING AREAS

Several participants admitted they either had no mission statement, or they supposedly had one but nobody believed in it anyway. In other words, those particular organizations are obviously paying only lip service instead of exhibiting true customer service.

One of the recurring, and rather alarming, themes was the answer to the statement: What is (are) the greatest problem(s) your organization faces today:
Answer: Governmental interference.
Other answers included:

Competition, especially from abroad
Increasing costs
Lack of vision and planning at the top
Growing too rapidly
Increased customer expectations
Not enough employee empowerment
Anticipating customers' future needs

Remember, many of the participants are in a rather precarious position--i.e., they have the vision, and they know what needs to be done within their respective organizations in order to improve customer service. They have been unable, however, to sell top management on the ideas. After all, old habits are difficult to break.

On the other hand, the top executives who participated in our survey have already been sold on the service concept or they believed in it already and caused it to permeate throughout the entire organization.

It is obviously much easier to establish a true customer service culture if the CEO believes in it than it is to sell the program "upward." Knowing that, I specifically questioned some of the participants about this phenomenon and I have included their responses in the subsequent chapter.

One participant even told me that although his company's policy was to practice excellent customer service, nobody in the company was free to discuss the company's policy or its mission statement. As a matter of fact, he wasn't even empowered to sign our survey. Kind of makes one wonder if top management believes in true customer service or if it is only paying lip service. What do you think?

EXPECTATIONS

As you might guess, our questionnaire was designed to reveal inconsistencies in participants' answers. The first two statements (see questionnaire in Figure 7-A) were expected to garner 4's or 5's, and not surprisingly, they generally did. (Only 13 respondents failed to answer with either a 4 or 5 on both of the first two statements). Responses on later statements in many cases, however, revealed that the organizations surveyed possibly do not exhibit the level of customer service which is purported by their slogans, buttons, and printed propaganda. Pie charts on the following pages succinctly illustrate some of the discrepancies we encountered.

Approximately one-half of the participants, however, exhibited consistency. In other words, not only did they purport to enjoy a customer service culture, they verified it with their answers.

So, since one-half of our participants actually demonstrate a true customer service culture, and since 10% returned the questionnaires, one might assume that only 5% (half of those who returned our surveys) of all the organizations in this country truly exhibit real customer service--the same percentage other researchers have found. One can assume, then, that the other 95% are paying only lip service. Is that surprising?

HYPOTHESIS

As a result of my studies, as well as my personal experiences, I concluded that the state of true customer service in this country was in shambles. The purpose of my survey was to ascertain whether or not I was correct. Unfortunately, I was proven correct.

The survey was designed in clusters with one or more similar statements comprising each cluster.

Cluster A (organizational commitment)	Statements 1 and 2
Cluster B (treatment of employees)	Statement 6
Cluster C (customer feedback and education)	Statements 7, 8, 9, an 10

ANALYSIS

It was relatively easy to glance at completed surveys as they reached us and then form cursory opinions.

For instance, if a survey respondent circled a high number on Cluster A (statements 1 and 2) and low numbers on statements 4 and 5, it was probably from an organization which generally demonstrates excellence in customer service.

Explanation: If an organization is <u>totally</u> committed to providing excellent customer service (1 and 2), then it would be logical to expect such an organization to not define quality as "conformance to requirements" (statement 4) nor to expect its employees to follow procedures in all customer service situations (statement 5).

Rather, such an organization would be more likely to define "quality" as it is defined by the customer. Also, employees could not be expected to follow procedures in all situations because a particular situation might dictate special handling.

Likewise, organizations which circled high numbers in Cluster A would logically circle high numbers in Clusters B and C. As you might guess, some of the questionnaires showed glaring inconsistencies.

SURVEY REVIEW

As I might have mentioned before, the purpose of sending out the questionnaire was to determine two things:

1. Does the subject organization profess to exhibit excellent customer service?
2. Does the subject organization actually exhibit excellent customer service? ---(or is it only lip service?)

The questionnaire was designed to ferret out the truth--i.e., it was difficult for respondents to cheat or to answer "like they thought I might want them to answer." So, while conceding that surveying 72 organizations hardly constitutes a scientific, error-free sample, it does serve as an indicator of the state of customer service in this country. And, incidentally, it quickly became painfully obvious that despite all that has been said and written about customer service and its advantages, it is still generally in sad shape.

There are shining exceptions, of course, and some of them are featured in the next chapter. Most of the organizations responding at least are attempting to improve their customer service practices. The real culprits are those which were too intimidated, disinterested, or confused even to respond to my questionnaire at all.

HERE'S HOW IT WORKS

(It is so important that you understand this section that you probably should read it again. If it still doesn't make sense, call me and I'll try to help).

We grouped sets of similar statements into "clusters." Then we compared other statements to those clusters to determine how consistent the respondents were with their answers.

Cluster A

Statement 1 (Our organization is totally committed to providing excellent customer service.)

Statement 2 (Our goal is to regularly exceed customer expectations.)

Cluster B

Statement 6 (We treat our employees as we expect them to treat our customers.)

Cluster C

Statement 7 (We regularly request feedback from our customers.)

Statement 8 (We utilize information from our customers to design our products and services.)

Statement 9 (We make it easy for customers to complain to us.)

Statement 10 (We educate our customers to most effectively utilize our products and services)

CLUSTER A

Statements 1 and 2 are closely related, so they comprise Cluster A:

1. Our organization is <u>totally</u> committed to providing excellent customer service.

2. Our goal is to regularly <u>exceed</u> customer expectations.

Not surprisingly, 92% of the respondents rated their organizations with a "4" (quite a bit) or with a "5" (exactly) on at least one of the first two statements. This group at least <u>professed</u> to exhibit excellent customer service. For simplicity, we'll refer to them as "wannabe's."

The remaining 8% admitted that they were lacking in their customer service practices ("1"--not at all, "2"--a little, and "3"--somewhat). This group <u>didn't even profess</u> to exhibiting excellent customer service. For simplicity, we'll refer to them as "don't wannabe's."

COMPARISONS

Let's go back to the 92% who rated themselves high on the customer service scale. One could reasonably expect them actually to practice excellent customer service. But do they? Not necessarily. Take a look at the relationship between their answers in Cluster A and other selected answers.

We specifically examined statements which were rated inconsistently by the respondents. In other words, just because these Cluster A respondents rated themselves positively doesn't necessarily mean they are "practicing what they preach."

Statement 5 (S-5) (Our employees are expected to follow procedures in all customer service situations)

I hoped that none, or at least very few respondents, would answer this statement affirmatively. Unfortunately, 40% of all respondents admitted to chaining their employees to rules, regulations, and procedures. See Figure 7-1.

Figure 7-1

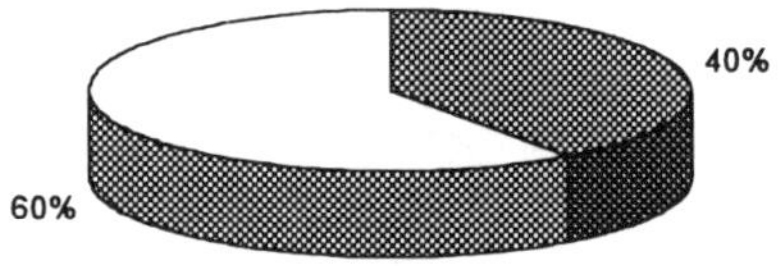

40% of all respondents expect their employees to follow rules, regulations, and procedures in all customer service situations.

* * * * * * * *

But worse than that, 44% of Cluster A's "wannabe's" also chain their employees to rules, regulations and procedures. See Figure 7-2.

Figure 7-2

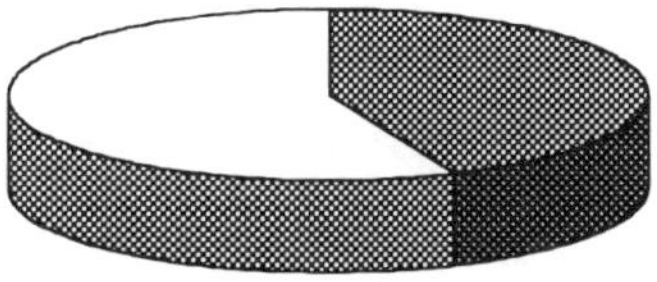

44% of Cluster A's "wannabe's" also expect their employees to follow rules, regulations, and procedures in all customer service situations.

Let's Tie It Up - S-5

These results represent an abhorrent situation. It's especially difficult for me to understand why almost one-half of the organizations which profess practicing excellent customer service actually fail to empower their employees. Instead, they expect their employees to follow "procedures" in all customer service situations. Ouch!

Statement 10 (S-10) (We educate our customers to most efficiently utilize our products and services)

Unlike my expectations on S-5, I expected a high percentage of respondents to answer affirmatively on this statement. However, as you can see in Figure 7-3, only 59% of all respondents did so.

Figure 7-3

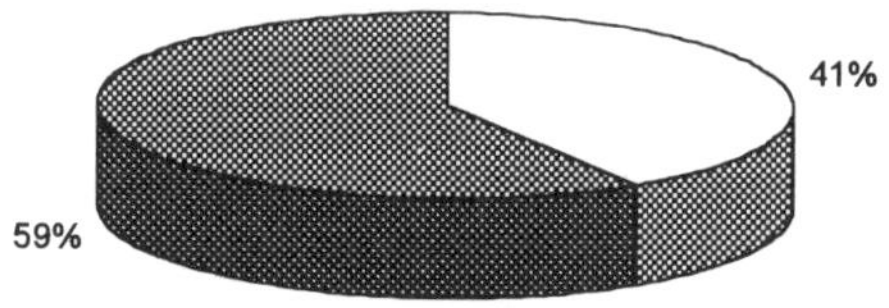

Only 59% of all respondents educate their customers to most effectively utilize their products and services.

* * * * * * * *

Almost as bad, though, only 65% of Cluster A's "wannabe's" educate their customers to effectively utilize their products and services. See Figure 7-4.

Figure 7-4

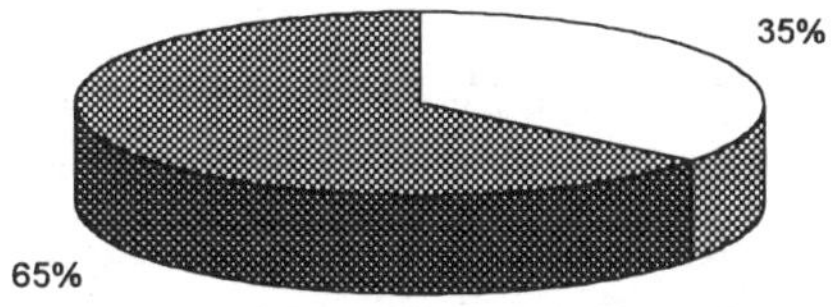

Only 65% of Cluster A's "wannabe's" educate their customers to most effectively utilize their products and services.

Let's Tie It Up - S-10

As you will observe in the next chapter, organizations which are totally committed to customer service are proactive rather than reactive. They anticipate their customers' problems rather than merely react to them, and many of those problems can be alleviated by properly educating customers. Similarly, they can utilize customer information to improve their products and services.

Statement 11 (S-11) (A part of each executive's job is direct customer contact)

Just when I thought it couldn't get any worse, it did! Progressive CEO's, presidents, and managers practice what Tom Peters calls "visible management." They escape from their ivory towers and occasionally rub elbows with the real money makers--their customers. You will read about such people in the next chapter.

A real shocker! Only 48% of all respondents could claim that part of their top executives' job was direct customer contact. See Figure 7-5.

Figure 7-5

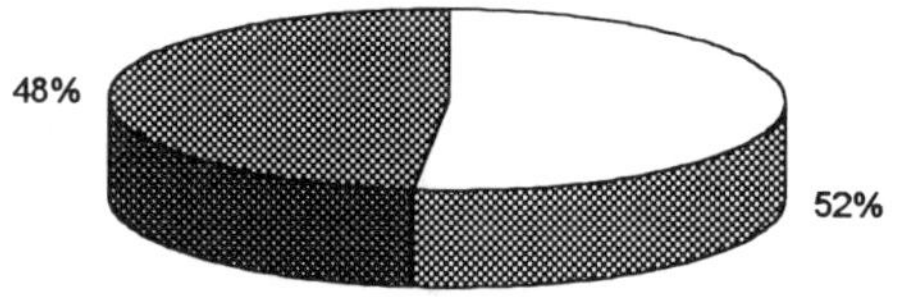

Only 48% of all respondents reported that part of their top executives' job was direct customer contact.

* * * * * * * *

Almost as bad was the reaction of the Cluster A "wannabe's." Only 53% of them are involved in direct customer contact. See Figure 7-6.

Firgure 7-6

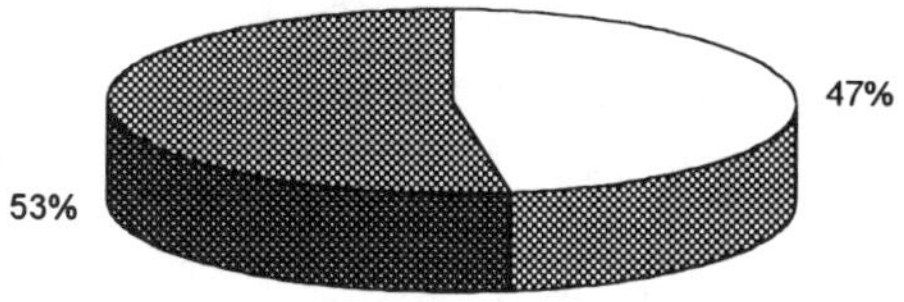

Only 53% of Cluster A's "wannabe's" say that part of their top executives' job is direct customer contact.

Let's Tie It Up - S-11

We all know how negative reports can become filtered as they pass upward through management levels. By the time they get to top management, they sometimes sound almost "positive." After all, no one wants to be a messenger of bad news. One of the most effective ways for top executives to know exactly what is going on is for them to find out themselves--by direct customer contact.

Statement 14 (S-14) (Employees are recognized and/or rewarded for "bending the rules" to meet a customer's needs)

My definition of "empowerment" is granting an employee the authority that matches responsibility. The most effective leaders empower their subordinates to take necessary actions in order to satisfy customers.

Yet only one-half of all respondents in our survey have seen fit to empower their employees adequately. See Figure 7-7.

Figure 7-7

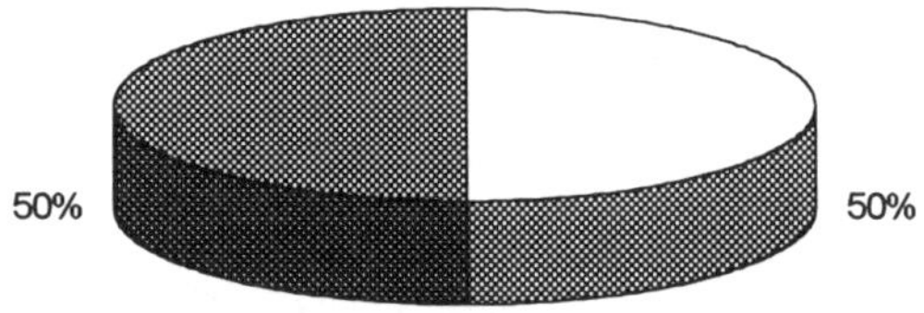

50% of all respondents recognize and/or reward their employees for "bending the rules" to meet a customer's needs.

* * * * * * * * *

Cluster A's "wannabe's" didn't fare much better. Only 54% of them are truly exhibiting excellent customer service in this respect. See Figure 7-8.

Firgure 7-8

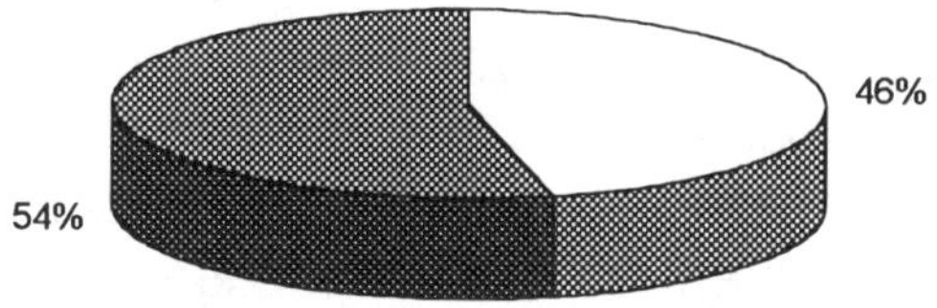

Only 54% of Cluster A's "wannabe's" recognize and/or reward their employees for "bending the rules" to meet a customer's needs.

Let's Tie It Up - S-14

It's beginning to look a lot like "lip service," isn't it? One of the best ways to empower employees is to "catch them in the act" of performing an extraordinary customer service function. Instant recognition and reward will reinforce them to repeat such an act.

Statement 15 (S-15) (All employees are routinely educated about our products and services)

It would be almost impossible for an organization to display excellent customer service without adequately training its employees. After all, it is these "front line" employees whom most customers contact, and upon whom most customers depend for information. Yet, a disappointingly low percentage of our total respondents seemed to think employees' knowledge was important--only 60%, to be exact. See Figure 7-9.

Figure 7-9

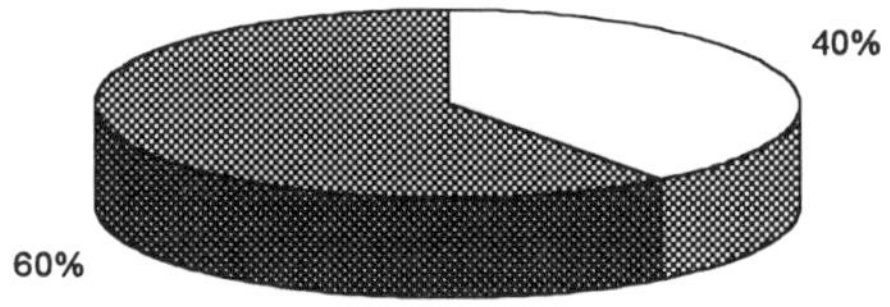

Only 60% of all respondents' employees are routinely educated about their products and services.

* * * * * * * *

Maybe one could expect such a low percentage for all respondents, but the truth is, only 65% of Cluster A's "wannabe's" recognize the importance of educating and training their employees. See Figure 7-10.

Figure 7-10

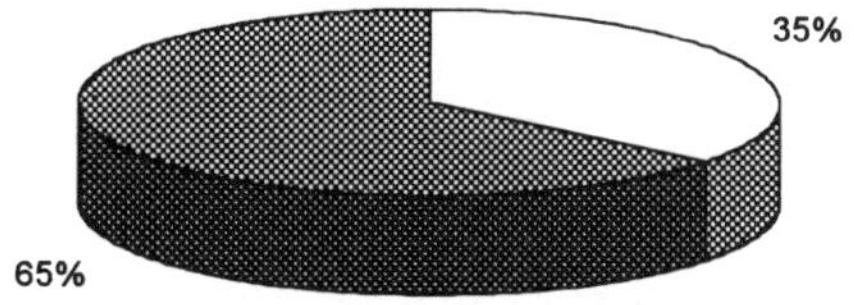

Only 65% of Cluster A's "wannabe's" routinely educate their employees about their products and services.

Let's Tie It Up - S-15

During my personal interviews with the "Top Ten," the recurring theme was that nothing is more vital to an organization's well-being than employee training. H.R. Chally, for instance, reminds us that the services surrounding a product are often more important than the product itself. Maintaining these services usually requires investments in "intellectual capital" in addition to the traditional capital investments in machinery and facilities. After all, in many cases, the only difference between some products is the people who sell them.

Consequently, it is difficult for me to believe an organization when it professes to exhibit excellence in customer service, and yet it ignores educating its employees.

Statement 16 (S-16) (All levels of employees have a say in how their jobs are performed and measured)

There are literally thousands of examples proving that employees perform more effectively if they have "bought in" to the process. We must remember that the people closest to the work know the most about the tasks of the job.

Consequently, they frequently have considerable insight into the intricacies of the process and can shed some light on process improvement. Most important, they will more likely perform effectively if they have a say, and a stake, in how a job is to be performed.

Yet, despite all of what has been written, spoken, and displayed about this subject, disappointingly few organizations give credence to the subject. Only 53% of all respondents allow their employees to have a say in how their jobs are performed and measured. See Figure 7-11.

Figure 7-11

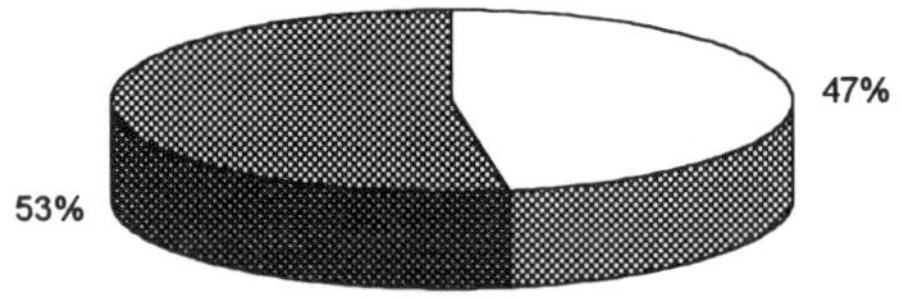

Only 53% of all respondents allow their employees to have a say in how their job is performed and measured.

* * * * * * * *

The "wannabe's" in Cluster A didn't fare much better. Only 57% of them allow their employees to have a say in how their job is performed and measured. See Figure 7-12.

Figure 7-12

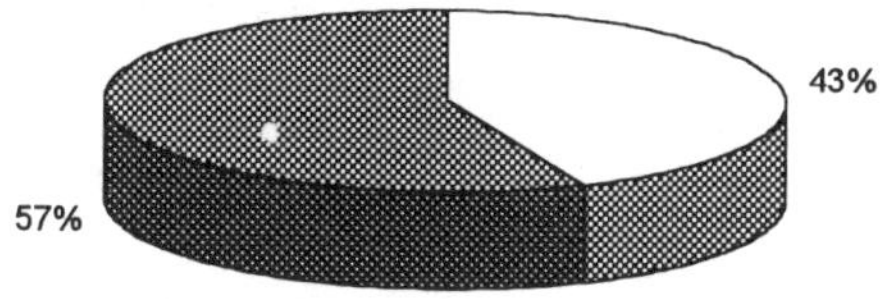

Only 57% of Cluster A's "wannabe's" allow their employees to have a say in how their job is performed and measured.

Let's Tie It Up - S-16

In I'm First: Your Customer's Message to You, Linda Silverman Goldzimer exhorts us to "Get everyone involved, so everyone has a vested interest in achieving your goals." In a customer-driven organization, everyone feels as if they <u>own</u> their job; they're not just renting it.

Just as in sales, people don't want to be <u>sold</u>; they want to be given an opportunity to <u>buy</u>. So, doesn't it make sense to create a culture which encourages employee input and participation? Your organization's success could very well depend on your treating your employees as <u>partners</u> instead of as pawns.

Statement 17 (S-17) (Our employees are cross-trained so they can fill in for each other)

While it is true we are in an age of specialization, I believe we need less single-dimensional, and more multiple-dimensional, employees. Few things are more irritating than calling a company for help or information and being told that "the only person knowledgeable in that area is on vacation for two weeks." What is the caller supposed to do in the meantime?

One respondent amplified his answer on this particular subject by blaming the union for not allowing cross-training. I wonder if it ever occurred to the union leadership how much more valuable (and secure) their members might be if they were more knowledgeable?

In any case, only 47% of all respondents cross-train their employees. It makes one wonder if the others have any training program at all. See Figure 7-13.

Figure 7-13

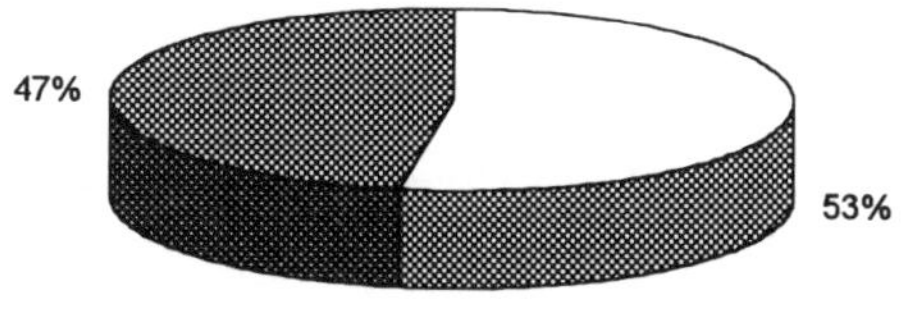

47% of all respondents cross-train their employees.

* * * * * * * *

Cluster A's "wannabe's" didn't set the world on fire either. Only 51% of them cross-train. The other half obviously doesn't. See Figure 7-14.

Figure 7-14

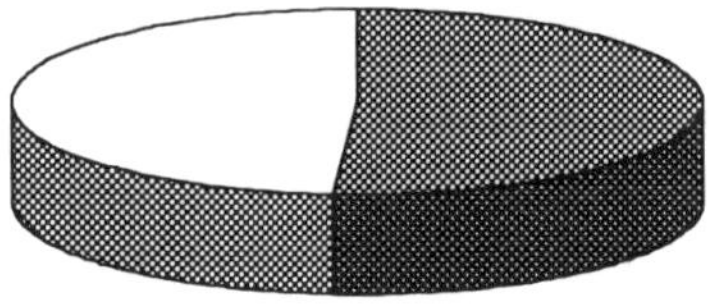

Only 51% of Cluster A's "wannabe's" cross-train their employees.

Let's Tie It Up - S-17

Logic dictates that the better rounded an employee becomes, the more valuable that employee becomes. I suspect many employees' "comfort zones" keep them from requesting cross-training. After all, they feel comfortable in their present positions and fear the unknown.

The problem is: who knows how long the present position will even exist? Isn't it logical that cross-training might lead to another position, one with better pay and more security? Specialization is fine, but single-dimensionalism is dangerous.

Statement 18 (S-18) (Employees do what it takes to help a customer even if it "isn't their job")

This aspect is closely related to the previous one, but it is also largely a matter of attitude and training. Unfortunately, the culprits who fall short in this endeavor are frequently near the top of the organization.

Unless they have been indoctrinated otherwise, some accountants, engineers, vice-presidents, security guards, and production managers simply don't understand why on earth they should be concerned with customer service. After all, they rarely have any direct contact with customers.

Remember, your job and your organization exists because of, and for, the customer. So no matter what your level or position, you must be ready and willing to step in if needed.

What would you do it your phone was ringing but no one was available to answer it? I'll tell you what I do: I answer it. It may not be my "job," but it could mean a lost sale if nobody answers.

Do you remember the concept of "moments of truth?" It occurs whenever anyone comes in contact with any aspect of your organization. It could be a newspaper ad, your storefront, your restrooms, a cashier, a busperson, or your vice-president of accounting hurriedly brushing past.

The culture of your organization should encourage, and even demand, that everyone does what it takes to help a customer even if it "isn't their job." Yet, only 61% of all respondents do so. See Figure 7-15.

Figure 7-15

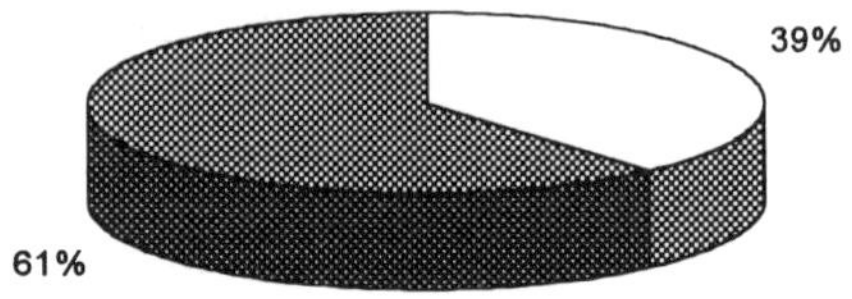

Only 61% of all respondents are organizations where employees do what it takes to help a customer, even if it isn't their job.

* * * * * * * *

Cluster A's "wannabe's" aren't much healthier. Only 67% of them are organizations where employees do what it takes to help a customer, even if it isn't their job. See Figure 7-16.

Figure 7-16

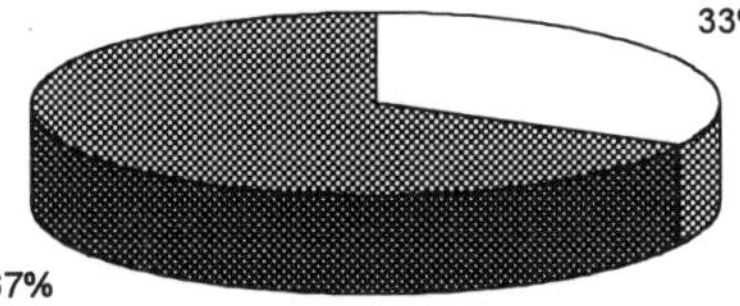

Only 67% of Cluster A's "wannabe's" are organizations where employees do what it takes to help a customer, even if it isn't their job.

Let's Tie It Up - S-18

Several years ago while heading through West Texas on a ski trip, our new Suburban broke down in San Angelo. It was Saturday morning and the Chevy dealer's service department was closed.

However, one of their mechanics just happened to be on the premises and offered to take a look at our car. He removed the starter, replaced a factory-defective pin, and had us back on the road in two hours.

You have no idea how grateful I was. I asked him how much I owed him and he replied, "Oh, nothing. I'm just glad I could help out."

I would have been glad to pay him hundreds of dollars! I finally persuaded him to take $50 for his unselfish and generous efforts. Can you believe it? This man helped us even though it "wasn't his job".

Statement 23 (S-23) (Departmental boundaries are intentionally invisible to the customer)

Most customers don't really care about your organizational structure, internal problems, setbacks, disappointments, or frustrations. All customers are interested in is: how well will you serve them?

Organizations must see themselves as a total package designed to serve their customers. Every department, division, and employee must learn to see the organization through the customer's eyes. While most of us agree, you would be surprised to see the number of raised eyebrows and gasps of disbelief when, during my seminars, I recommend eliminating out-dated customer service departments.

The fact is, <u>everyone</u> in an organization is responsible for ensuring excellence in customer service. Remember, a chain is only as strong as its weakest link. Similarly, an organization is only as strong as its weakest employee--no matter which department he or she occupies.

Yet, a startling few of our respondents have killed their dinosaurs and evolved to today's needs. Only 36% of all respondents reported that their department boundaries are invisible to the customer. See Figure 7-17.

Figure 7-17

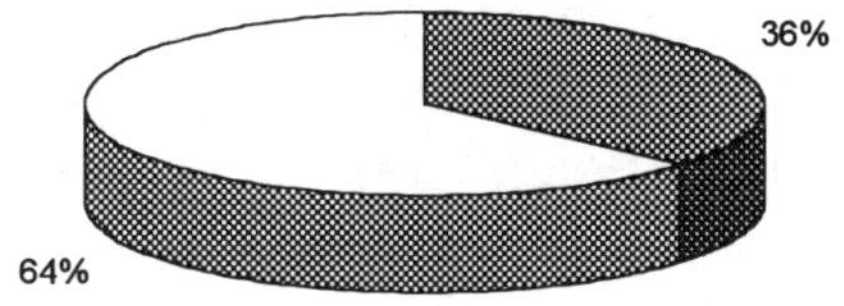

Only 36% of all respondents reported that their departmental boundaries are invisible to the customer.

* * * * * * * *

One certainly would expect almost a unanimous elimination of visible departmental boundaries from Cluster A's "wannabe's." Unfortunately, however, only <u>39%</u> of them reported affirmatively. See Figure 7-18.

Figure 7-18

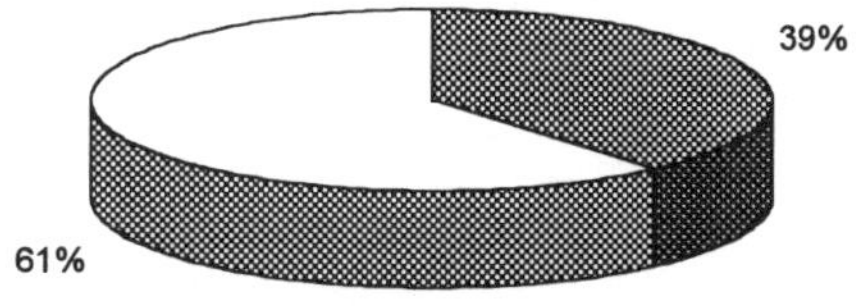

Departmental boundaries are intentionally invisible to the customer in only 39% of Cluster A's "wannabe's."

Let's Tie It Up - S-23

When it comes to winning and keeping customers, it's the customer's perception of the quality of service that determines how successful your organization will be. It's not the quality of service you give, but the quality of service the customer perceives which makes the difference.

Nothing is more disgusting than to observe in-fighting or blame-throwing between departments. Just as on an athletic team, once its participants begin arguing, they have already begun to lose.

Do you think a customer really cares whose fault a problem is--sales', engineering's, or accounting's? Our only concern should be to exceed our customers' expectations--not to build departmental dynasties.

Statement 24 (S-24) (Teamwork is rewarded above individual accomplishment)

Few techniques of management have caused more excitement lately than the creation of teams to establish a direction, share information, and solve problems. The hierarchical world of organization charts, formal information flow and "channels" should already be a thing of the past.

In the past, the boss made the decisions, which usually were then force-fed down the line. In more "progressive" organizations, attempts were made to motivate employees into accepting top management's views. But, hey, aren't two, or three, or six, or even ten heads better than one? Why not take advantage of all those heads and utilize teams in planning situations?

There exist situations in which there is not enough time for a team approach in solving problems. However, I believe teams can solve numerous potential problems by avoiding them in the first place.

Yet only a small percentage of our respondents employ the teamwork concept. Only 38% of all respondents reward teamwork above individual accomplishment. See Figure 7-19.

Figure 7-19

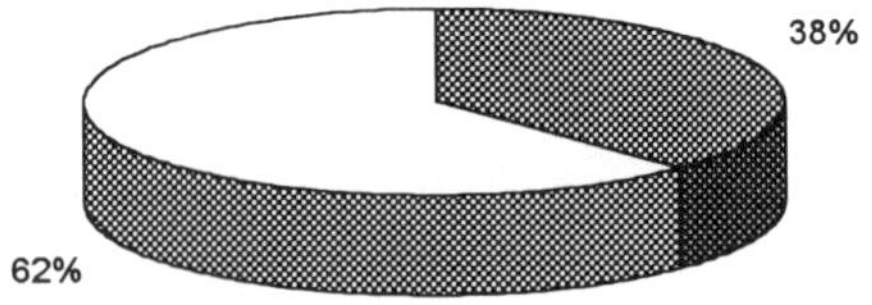

Only 38% of all respondents reward teamwork above individual accomplishment.

* * * * * * * *

Surely, I thought, most of Cluster A's "wannabe's" subscribe to the team approach in setting policy and solving problems. However, I couldn't have been more incorrect. Only 42% of them reward teamwork above individual accomplishment. See Figure 7-20.

Figure 7-20

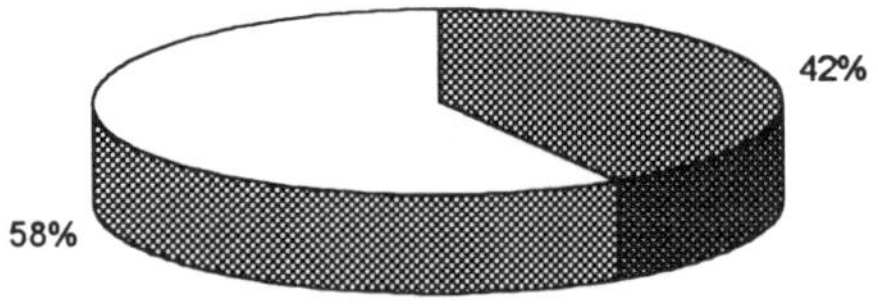

Only 42% of Cluster A's "wannabe's" reward teamwork over individual accomplishment.

Let's Tie It Up - S-24

I am not advocating conducting business by "committee." We have all been subjected to attending boring committee meetings which accomplished absolutely nothing.

What I am advocating, however, is the spirit of teamwork--working together, not apart. Just as the one-night stand is obsolete in the sales field, the lone-wolf concept is obsolete in the management arena.

Some of the best ideas dealing with customer service will originate from front-line employees, if only we include them on our team.

Statement 25 (S-25) (Our organization department heads work together to eliminate mistakes and defects before they occur)

This concept is closely related to Q-17 (cross-training), Q-23 (invisible departmental boundaries), and Q-24 (teamwork). However, I thought it worthwhile to address it separately to illustrate the arrogance of many departmental empires.

It makes sense to work together, but personal and professional jealousies often prevent common sense from prevailing. As you can see, only 57% of all respondents' department heads cooperate in advance with one another. See Figure 7-21.

Figure 7-21

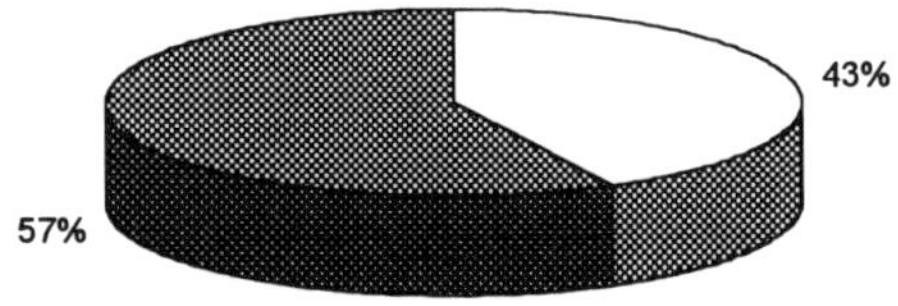

Only 57% of all respondents' department heads work together to eliminate mistakes and defects before they occur.

* * * * * * * *

Cluster A's "wannabe's" didn't fare much better. Only 62% of their department heads work together to eliminate mistakes and defects before they occur. See Figure 7-22.

Figure 7-22

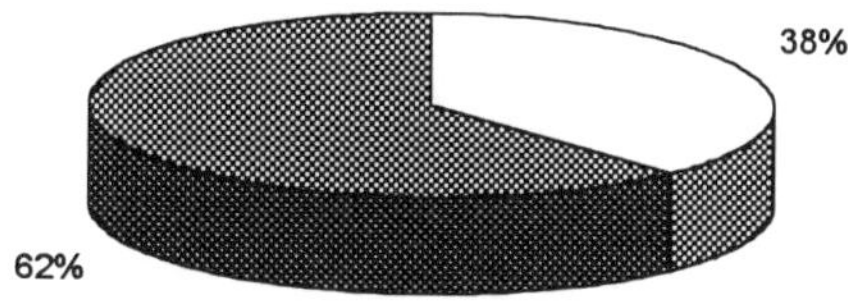

Only 62% of Cluster A's "wannabe's" department heads work together to eliminate mistakes before they occur.

Let's Tie It Together - S-25

I believe the Cluster A inconsistencies illustrated are especially significant. As stated earlier, 92% of Cluster A respondents claimed to practice excellent customer service. However, as you have seen by reviewing the results of additional questionnaire statements, what many organizations profess to do isn't necessarily what they do.

CLUSTER A IN PERSPECTIVE

I'm afraid these results are indicative of exactly what's happening in our country today. Maybe you're right: There probably <u>are</u> enough customer service books available. Now if we could only get everyone to <u>read</u> 'em.

CLUSTER B

Statement 6 is so important that we elected to consider it by itself.

Statement 6 (S-6) (We treat our employees as we expect them to treat our customers)

If you're not directly serving the customer, you'd better be serving someone who is. Your employees are your internal customers. It is they who will ultimately determine the success or failure of your organization.

Unless the culture of your organization is obsessed with its employees, it's merely mocking customer service. It's not possible to have one without the other.

In most cases, the front-line employee IS your organization, as far as the ultimate customer is concerned. Yet, many organizations are remiss when it comes to training, recognizing, and rewarding those front-line warriors.

Approximately 75% of Cluster B respondents answered Statement 6 with a "4" (quite a bit) or a "5" (describes it exactly). Again, as before, we will refer to them as Cluster B "wannabe's." Those who answered with a "1," "2," or a "3" will be referred to as "don't wannabe's."

Let's examine some selected discrepancies in Cluster B's answers.

Statement 14 (S-14) (Employees are recognized and/or rewarded for "bending the rules" to meet a customer's needs)

There is a major discrepancy here. On the one hand, the majority of Cluster B respondents claim to "treat their employees as we expect them to treat our customers;" yet only 46% of all respondents recognize their employees for "bending the rules" to meet a customer's needs. See Figure 7-23.

Figure 7-23

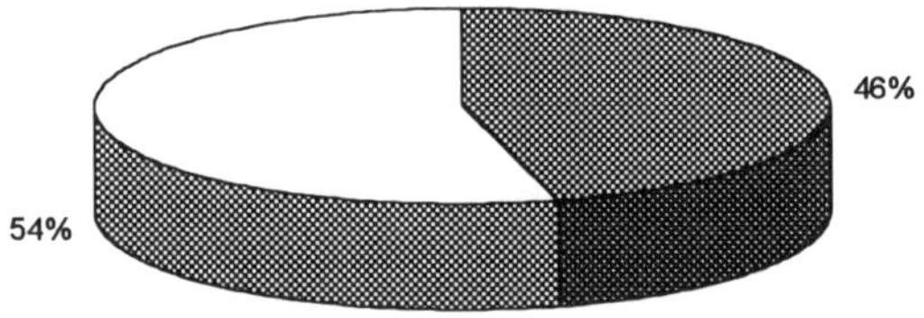

Only 46% of all respondents recognize their employees for "bending the rules" to meet a customer's needs.

* * * * * * * * *

Unfortunately, Cluster B's "wannabe's" didn't do much better. See Figure 7-24.

Figure 7-24

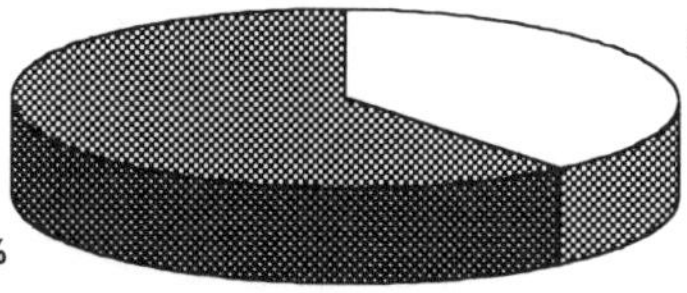

Only 61% of Cluster B's "wannabe's" recognize and/or reward their employees for "bending the rules" to meet a customer's needs.

Let's Tie It Up - S-14

Someone is being less than truthful. There is nothing more discouraging to an employee than being reprimanded for making a decision, unless it's not being allowed to make a decision. There are thousands of events occurring daily which managers don't even know about--or need to know about, so why bother them with every little decision?

If you have an effective hiring procedure in place, and if your training and education programs are adequate, then you should feel safe in empowering your employees to do what it takes to satisfy customers. It shouldn't be necessary to stroke a manager's ego by requiring him or her to make every little decision.

Statement 19 (S-19) (The first criteria for promotion is customer service, whether internal or external customers)

Until organizations "put their money where their mouths are" they will continue paying lip service instead of displaying customer service. In all too many cases, the very same organizations which claim to treat their employees as they want their employees to treat their customers, turn their backs when promotion time comes around.

Only 40% of all respondents really promote their employees as a result of their customer service actions. See Figure 7-25

Figure 7-25

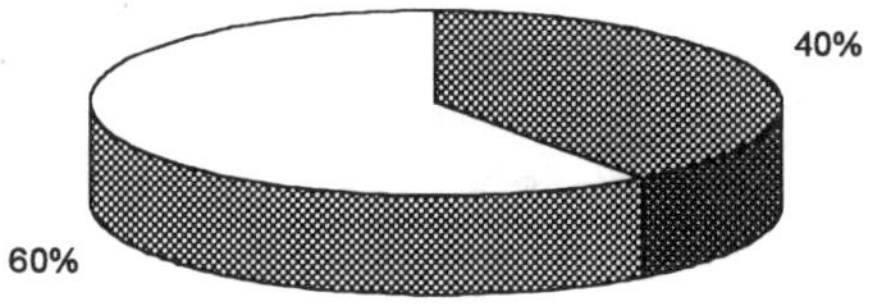

Only 40% of all respondents consider their employees' customer service actions as the first criteria for promotion.

* * * * * * * *

Well, what about Cluster B's "wannabe's?" Are they practicing what they preach? No, not really. Only 53% of them come through for their employees. See Figure 7-26.

Figure 7-26

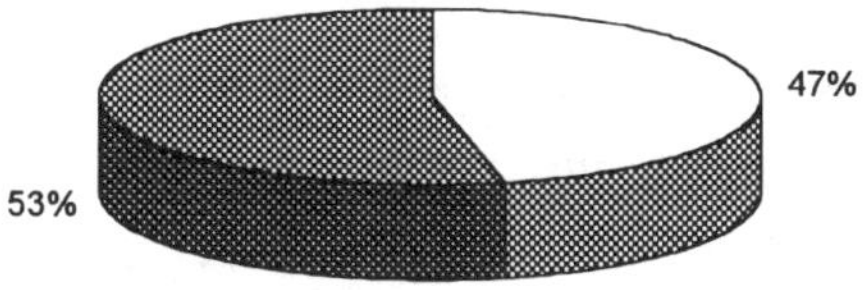

Only 53% of Cluster B's "wannabe's" say the first criteria for promotion is customer service.

Let's Tie It Together - S-19

What message do you think employees are receiving today? Does it appear as if being obsessed with excellent customer service creates a pathway to the top? Not really. It appears as if production, engineering, and sales, as well as every other department, has an inside track.

CLUSTER B IN PERSPECTIVE

Most of us will agree that the success or failure of any organization heavily depends upon its employees. Also, most of us will agree that excellent customer service will provide an organization with the competitive edge.

It seems so simple, then, that when an employee exhibits excellent customer service practices and helps ensure our success, he or she should be duly recognized, rewarded, and at least be considered for promotion and advancement.

CLUSTER C

Cluster C is comprised of four closely related statements. They all deal with the organization's relationship to the customer, so they are especially important. The following statements comprise this cluster:

Statement 7 (S-7) (We regularly request feedback from our customers)

Statement 8 (S-8) (We utilize information from our customers to design our products and services)

Statement 9 (S-9) (We make it easy for customers to complain to us)

Statement 10 (S-10) (We educate our customers to most efficiently utilize our products and services)

A whopping 97% of our respondents rated themselves a "4" or a "5" (wannabe's) on this cluster. After all, it would be extremely difficult to stay in business if an organization failed to communicate with its customers, wouldn't it?

Let's review some selected discrepancies in Cluster C's responses.

Statement 11 (S-11) (A part of each executive's job is direct customer contact)

One of the first actions that San Antonio's new police chief, Al Phillipus, took was to don his uniform and ride with his officers. During his first week as the new chief he even helped diffuse a hostage situation.

In my opinion, he accomplished at least three important objectives:

1. He was able to observe first hand the problems his police force faces.
2. He was able to rub elbows with some of his "customers" (the public).
3. He gained additional respect and admiration from both his police force and from the public.

What a great idea, right? Why don't more executives do what Chief Phillipus is doing? Reviewing reports in your office is a poor substitute for getting the facts first hand.

After being led to believe that Cluster C has 97% "wannabe's," it was disappointing to learn that only half of all respondents' top executives conduct direct customer contact. See Figure 7-27.

Figure 7-27

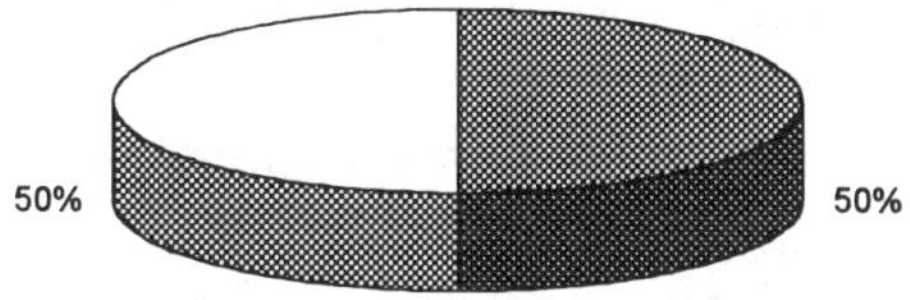

Only 50% of all respondents make direct customer contact part of their top executives' job.

* * * * * * * *

How did the "wannabe's" do? Not much better. Only 51% of them make direct customer contact part of their top executives' job. See Figure 7-28.

Figure 7-28

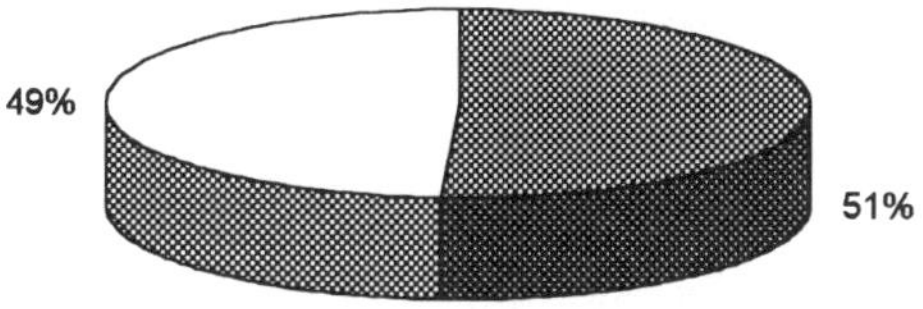

Only 51% of the "wannabe's" make direct customer contact part of their top executives" job.

Let's Tie It Up - S-11

Somebody's not telling the truth. How can almost everyone claim he or she places the customer first, yet only half make direct customer contact part of their top executives' job?

Progressive organizations today are fleeing from the old top-down, pyramid organization chart. Invert the pyramid and you will see who the boss really is: it's the customer. It behooves us to make sure that our top executives know what customers' needs are. And there is no better way than to ask them directly.

Statement 15 (S-15) (All employees are routinely educated about our products and services)

It is rare that a customer will call or write top management with a complaint, question, or suggestion. Customers usually wait to take such actions only after all other avenues have been exhausted.

Most customers will, instead, contact a front-line employee or someone else who happens to be available at the time. You can understand, then, why it is so important to have informed, educated employees in your organization.

Yet, only 63% of all Cluster C respondents reported that they regularly educate their employees about their products and services. See Figure 7-29.

Figure 7-29

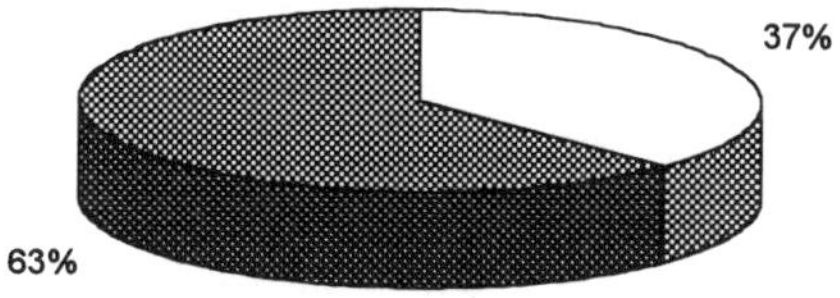

Only 63% of all respondents routinely educate all their employees about their products and services.

* * * * * * * *

Certainly, I thought, the "wannabe's" would score much higher. Wrong! Only 64% of them routinely educate all their employees about their products and services. See Figure 7-30.

Figure 7-30

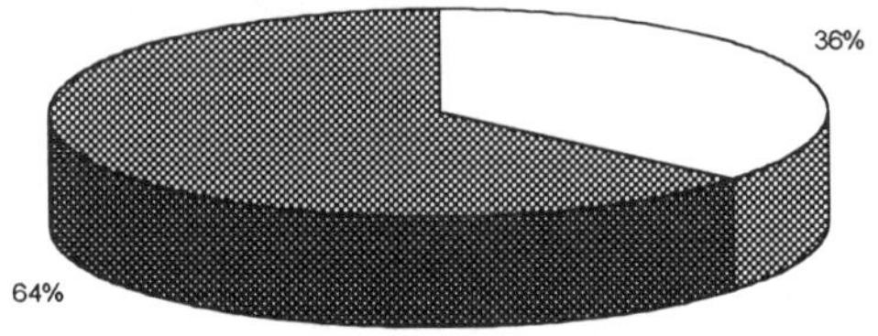

Only 64% of Cluster C "wannabe's" routinely educate all their employees about their products and services.

Let's Tie It Up - S-15

As I mentioned before, "moments of truth" may occur at any time. Whenever a customer comes in contact with one of your employees, wouldn't it be nice if that customer came away favorably impressed?

The answer, of course, is "yes." And one of the best ways to ensure it happens in this manner is to make sure all of your employees are trained, educated, and knowledgeable.

CLUSTER C IN PERSPECTIVE

Only two statements were examined in Cluster C, but their significance is astounding.

In order for an organization actually to educate, to obtain feedback, and to receive complaints and suggestions from its customers, it is vital that two principles are in place:

1. A part of each executive's job should be direct customer contact.

2. All employees should be routinely educated about your products and services.

THE QUESTIONNAIRE STUDY IN PERSPECTIVE

As I mentioned at the outset of this chapter, our study was designed to verify our hypothesis: The state of true customer service in this country is in shambles.

I had heard it. I had read it. Now I have verified it.

Despite the fact that so many pay lip service to it, so few are obsessed with customer service. The selected comparisons we examined certainly bear witness to that conclusion.

It is also a fact, however, that excellent customer service gives an organization more than just a competitive weapon. It's a survival skill. It's not just a competitive edge. It's THE competitive edge.

While many of the results were disappointing, many were encouraging. Whenever one-half are not performing as they profess, the other one-half obviously are.

There were numerous bright, shining examples of successful organizations which practice exactly what they preach. Ten of them are highlighted in the next chapter.

8 TOP TEN INTERVIEWS

Although most survey participants included their mission statements, and some even sent copies of testimonial letters they have received from satisfied customers, ten of the participants particularly stand out and deserve special recognition. This chapter will feature their mission statements, an analysis of their responses, and excerpts of my personal interviews with them. These participants will be discussed in alphabetical order. Each of them has been generous with their time, and I am most appreciative for their cooperation.

AAA POTOMAC

The first item which greeted me when I received AAA Potomac's response was a business-size plastic card with AAA's mission statement printed on it: "Five Diamond service is our commitment to meet, and preferably to exceed, each member's need by rendering friendly, polite and error-free service as quickly as possible every time. An attitude of `close enough' is never acceptable."

Wow! Do they mean it? Evidently so, because included in the response were copies of letters to and from customers. Let me include just a paragraph from one of them: "Before I cash in the dues paying check to renew our AAA membership, I wanted to reply to your letter. Many people these days only take the time to complain and not to come back and say `thank you' for a job extremely well done. Thanks again for your professional and thorough response."

BALDRIDGE CRITERIA

During my personal interview with Ms. Cecilia Quattromani, Manager of Member Relations for AAA Potomac, I learned that her company sincerely believes in providing excellence in customer service. They believe in it so much, in fact, that they utilize Baldridge Award criteria in their operations. (The Malcolm Baldridge National Quality Award, modeled after the

Deming Prize, was established by the U.S. Congress in 1987 to recognize those organizations each year--a maximum of six--who demonstrate excellence in quality management).

Empowerment is a key ingredient, according to Ms. Quattromani. When I asked her what advice she could give to other companies when they attempt to embark on a true customer service program, she simply reminded me to remember that "the customer is always right." She went on to say that misunderstandings can occur when the customer isn't properly educated about a product or service. Also, utilizing tact and even "giving in" is better than winning the argument.

While many of us are fortunate enough to work in an organization which already believes in true customer service, what about those who aren't so lucky? How does one go about convincing management, or even fellow employees, that excellent customer service really pays off?

She advises to begin in a small way. Don't try to solve the entire company's problems all at once. Begin in your own department, with your own employees. Positive outcomes as a result of changing your customer service practices will garner attention at all levels. Set the example, even if you have to do it all by yourself.

AMOCO OIL COMPANY

It was obvious from the start that Amoco enjoys a customer service culture. But had it always been so? Not necessarily.

I asked Mr. Rudy Marcinko, Manager of Credit Card Customer Service, how the company began forming a customer service culture. Had it always been present, or had an event triggered the movement?

In 1987, Amoco found it necessary to reduce expenses. Consequently, it conducted an in-depth investigation of every function performed within the company. As a result, the company began focusing on the work process and asking the question, "What is your role within this process?"

Department walls were torn down and, over time, the emphasis shifted from a "product" culture to a "service" culture. It became obvious that Amoco needed to understand its work processes, design around customer needs, and remain close to the customer.

The greatest difficulty to overcome when instituting such a program? Communicating it to every employee. Management tried to be "up front" with everyone, yet some employees simply didn't buy into the new movement. Mr. Marcinko reiterated exactly what I've been hearing from almost everyone: the movement must begin at the senior level; everyone must be involved; and everyone must be given the opportunity to provide input. If not, the program simply won't get off the ground.

"What's the best way to convince fellow workers about the benefits of customer service culture?" Walk the talk; set the example. (Tom Peters calls it "visible management"). Reward people for practicing excellence in customer service.

Amoco Oil Company attributes its performance success to five major aspects: strategy, work processes, organizational structure, rewards and recognition, and people. Most important--people.

Their mission statement:

Surprise and delight our customers by exceeding our customers' expectations through personalized customer service at a competitive cost. This will be achieved by:

- *Satisfying our customer requirements.*
- *Exceeding customers' expectations.*
- *Maximizing production through full participation and empowerment of trained/motivated employees.*
- *Competitive benchmarking.*

One of the most interesting and enlightening responses on Amoco's questionnaire was the answer to the question "Who are your internal customers?" (Many companies don't know).

Amoco knows. "Anyone that you hand off a process to." That more or less includes everyone in the company, doesn't it?

My gratitude to Amoco, and especially to Mr. Rudy Marcinko, for his insight and for being so generous with his time.

BASS PRO SHOPS

I must admit that prior to this project I had never heard of Bass Pro Shops, and when I saw them on the list to be surveyed, I wondered just how much we could learn from a "bait stand." Well, I learned very quickly that this outfit wasn't just a "bait stand," but instead, it was a highly professional organization which caters to customers all over the country.

Their response included not only the completed questionnaire, but also brochures, background information, copies of testimonial letters, and even a video. Needless to say, I was impressed.

Then, to top it all off, my wife and I had the opportunity to visit the Bass Pro Shops and we came away even more impressed. We especially enjoyed the underwater fish-feeding show, not to mention the 140,000 gallon aquarium system, trout pond, four-story natural stone waterfall, and 150,000 square feet of boats, rods and reels, lures, wildlife art gallery, and gift shop. We spent several hours there and hated to leave.

Mr. Arley M. Clark, Director of Catalog Services, was kind enough to include Bass Pro Shop's mission statement:

> *To be the leading merchant of outdoor recreational products by offering our catalog, retail, destination, and wholesale customers exceptional value through a combination of low prices, large selection,*

top quality, and superior service. This will be enhanced by our Associates' merchandise expertise and reflects our concern for the well-being of our customers, suppliers, and associates, and conservation of our natural environment.

That kind of sums it up, doesn't it?

Not quite! This organization doesn't simply sell products and then treats those customers "right." It has created a whole customer service culture. Bass Pro Shops' founder, John L. Morris, has served as chairman of the National Fish and Wildlife Foundation, is on the Board of Trustees of the International Game Fish Association, and is currently serving as the Honorary Chairman of Fund Raising for the University of Missouri's School of Forestry, Fishery and Wildlife's $13 million center.

His additional awards and recognition include:

- 1993 Master Conservationist Award from the Missouri Department of Conservation.
- 1992 Fisherman of the Year Award from the Sport Fishing Institute.
- 1990 recipient of the Teddy Roosevelt Conservationist Award, presented by former President George Bush.

Need I go on? The founder, the company, and the employees live, work, and breathe customer service. You can tell when you walk into the place.

TESTIMONIALS

I have taken the liberty of including several excerpts from letters Mr. Clark shared with me:

> " This letter could go on for 10 pages with compliments and praise. The bottom line is to thank you and your employees for a great job...."
>
> "I am writing to Thank You...."
>
> "This time, you've really outdone yourself and made my weekend much more enjoyable. My hat's off to all of you. Thank you for being a company that services people."
>
> "I am writing to compliment you for the prompt attention given to my first order with Bass Pro Shops."
>
> "It is extremely pleasing, especially in this day, to find a company that not only practices customer service but that lives it each and every business day."

I could go on and on because there were many more letters included in Mr. Clark's package. But I think you've gotten the picture by now. Let's proceed to my interview with Mr. Clark.

INTERVIEW

One of my questions for Arley Clark was, "What were the greatest difficulties to overcome when you began your customer service program?" He succinctly summed it up: cost and convincing everyone to change.

Have you ever heard that before? Almost everyone agrees with the concept of excellence in customer service, but when it needs to be paid for, many fade from the picture. How much is it worth? Too much not to do it; that's how much.

Can you convince everybody to change? No way. Everyone is inherently resistant to change. "I've been doing this for 30 years and nobody is going to tell me to do it differently now."

When asked what advice he could give to businesses or employees when they try to institute a real customer service program, Mr. Clark remarked, "Tell them to put on the customer's hat. How would they feel if they were the customer and were dealing with you?"

Another suggestion was to call your competitors. Listen to how they answer the phone. (During the phone-handling segment of my seminars I usually give participants the opportunity to call their companies and have the conversation amplified so all seminar participants can hear it. Few are willing to call their own companies. I wonder why).

Mr. Clark reminded me that change is inevitable and we must conduct business differently than we did yesterday. "Plant the seeds," he said. "Look at what the competition is doing. Then you can convince your boss, your employees, and your co-workers that we must employ customer service excellence."

Mr. Clark, and Bass Pro Shops, I appreciate your time, information and expertise. It's no wonder that you're successful.

BROWN AND SHARPE MANUFACTURING COMPANY

My interview with this fine organization was a bit unusual. Not only did I have the opportunity to interview Ms. Penny Panebianco, the present Customer Service Supervisor, but also her former supervisor, Mr. Russ Hassler, who is now with another company.

The reason? Ms. Panebianco attributed much of Brown and Sharpe's customer service success to Mr. Hassler, who actually initiated and engineered dramatic changes at Brown and Sharpe while he was employed there.

Both individuals agreed how their customer service program began. Basically, it began when the work flow was changed from a "paper" focused process to a "computer" focused process. How did this help? It saved a lot of time so the company could focus more time on their customers.

What were the greatest difficulties to overcome? Changing the mindset of upper management from being merely "bottom-line" oriented to becoming customer-service oriented. That strikes a familiar chord, doesn't it?

So how did it all begin? Well, it seems Mr. Hassler had been in sales approximately four years and was complaining about the state of customer service. His CEO gave him the green light to "fix it."

The only reason his suggestions and ideas worked is because he had the CEO's "ear." Unless top management can be sold on the customer service concept, it will never fly in any organization.

When asked "What's the best way to convince co-workers about the benefits of becoming obsessed with customer service?," the answer was similar to what I heard from every organization: <u>education</u>. The customer service department invited other departments within the company to attend demonstrations in order to convince them customer-focused processes really work. Even though you "know" customer focusing really works, you must be able to prove your case.

How are customers able to complain or make suggestions to Brown and Sharpe? The company maintains a 1-800 number customers can use. A call is returned, at the latest, the next business day.

MISSION STATEMENT

> We will provide superior quality products, on time, and in accordance with the requirements specified by our customers. Each delivery shall create a recommendation for further business. It shall be the daily nature of our business that every employee will perform in a manner which promotes the continuous improvement of our processes, products and services.

OBSERVATIONS

It was evident from the outset that this company was refreshingly unusual, especially since so many manufacturing companies focus on process rather than on customers. However, the returned questionnaire told a different story for this company.

Furthermore, the fact that Ms. Panebianco credited much of the company's success to someone who is no longer even employed by the company, told me that a certain progressive spirit prevails within this organization. My hat is off to the management and employees, and my gratitude to both Ms. Panebianco and to Mr. Hassler is heartfelt.

THE COPPS CORPORATION

Two items grabbed my attention when I reviewed the questionnaire from Copps. First, the questionnaire answers were almost "textbook," and second, the mission statement was short and to the point.

Ms. Judy Ordens, Director of Consumer Affairs, completed the questionnaire for me, but I was fortunate enough to be able to personally interview Mr. Tom Copps, Executive Vice-President of Public Relations. It is always enlightening to have the opportunity to receive input from more than one individual within an organization, and this was no exception.

Whereas no particular event necessitated the philosophy of customer focus, the mere fact that Copps is somewhat smaller than some of its competitors forced it to become better than its competitors. Consequently, it focuses on upscale stores--the kind of customers who are more discerning and particular.

One of the greatest difficulties to overcome in this, or any organization which employs numerous part-timers, is the ability to motivate them. Copps helps solve this problem by attempting to make their employees feel as if they have a real stake in the operation of the company. For instance, when a young person is hired, a letter is sent to the new employee's parents, congratulating them and the employee.

When asked what advice he would offer to a business or employee trying to institute a customer service philosophy, Mr. Copps stressed that such a movement must be from the top down. Every organization interviewed agreed that unless top management believes in true customer focus, it will only occur sporadically within the organization. (That's why I insist on top management attending my customer service seminars along with their employees).

One of the really bright spots in the Copps program is its regular consumer group meetings during which time consumers share their concerns and suggestions. When asked, "What did you like most about the consumer advisory board meetings?," one consumer replied, "The information shared by everyone, including the store managers. I would never have thought to ask if I wanted something or told them I was dissatisfied. I would have just stopped coming."

"I feel Copps was very responsive to our comments. They made changes whenever possible on products and services offered. I feel they helped me to be a better consumer, plus I have to admit, I am a firm believer of Copps now. Thank you for letting me serve on your board. Copps certainly knows how to treat the customer."

MISSION STATEMENT

To create a uniquely satisfying shopping experience in which customers are offered products and services that exceed their expectations.

I like it! It's short, sweet, and to the point. I want to express my gratitude to both Ms. Judy Ordens and to Mr. Tom Copps for generously sharing their time and thoughts with me. With attitudes like theirs, it's easy to see why The Copps Corporation is successful.

DIAMOND SHAMROCK, INC.

The April 1, 1995, business section of the San Antonio Express-News headlines read, "Shamrock Selects Headquarters Site." Diamond Shamrock, Inc. will soon begin building a 200,000-square-foot corporate headquarters on a 148-acre tract in northwest San Antonio.

Roger Hemminghaus, chairman, chief executive, and president, estimated combined cost of the land and construction of the campus-like headquarters at $20 million.

"As a major employer, we want to provide a very attractive and functional facility for our people--our key resource," said Hemminghaus. "This new location will position our company to continue to attract and retain the very best employees and provide ample room for expansion," he said.

Diamond Shamrock, a Fortune 500 firm with sales of over $2.5 billion, is experiencing significant growth throughout Texas, Colorado, Louisiana, and New Mexico. It employs around 6,500 people.

It was a pleasure for me to receive a completed questionnaire from Mr. Hemminghaus, and even more of a pleasure to conduct a personal interview with him. It was immediately clear why Diamond Shamrock is successful. The company emphasizes its people.

According to Mr. Hemminghaus, the company really began emphasizing Total Quality Management

(TQM) in 1990. As a result of its emphasis on quality systems and customer concern, the company's retail income tripled during the next four years.

Since then, Diamond Shamrock has focused on three major areas:

1. Training of its employees.
2. Recognition of customer service excellence.
3. Middle management support.

The latter (middle management support) was of particular interest to me. Most of the other interviewees stressed the importance of top management's support of customer service programs. This time, I was talking to top management, and he emphasized that no one person or position can make the total difference. It takes everyone, up and down the line to make such a program viable.

When asked how a person within an organization can convince others about the advantages of becoming obsessed with customer service, Mr. Hemminghaus simply stated, "Get the CEO to attend a seminar on customer service, or at least get the CEO to talk with other CEO's about their successes."

MISSION STATEMENT

> *As a cohesive team we will grow and achieve superior financial results for our company. We will consistently:*

- *Focus on our customers.*
- *Improve everything we do.*
- *Produce quality products and services.*
- *Out-perform competition.*
- *Create opportunities out of change.*
- *Value, respect, and develop every employee.*
- *Encourage each employee's participation and ideas.*
- *Be ethical, responsible, and protective of the environment.*
- *Be safe, have fun, and take pride in our work.*

I wish to express my gratitude to Mr. Roger Hemminghaus for his time, for his comments, and for his vision. He and his organization are a tribute to San Antonio and to the nation.

FEDERAL EXPRESS

My questionnaire provided respondents an opportunity to describe a favorite customer service success story. As one might expect, Federal Express had such a story to share.

One of their couriers, who had temporarily taken over a route for another courier who was ill, misplaced the key to a Federal Express dropbox (the kind you see in building lobbies or on the street). Rather than falling behind schedule, he "walked" the 500-pound metal box over to his van, pushed it in, and drove it back to his station where it could be opened and the packages removed. Those customers' important shipments were not going to be late!

Federal Express Corporation has developed a reputation for excellent customer service, and as a result of its questionnaire and my personal interview, I can understand why. Ms. Jean H. Ward-Jones, Manager of Corporate Quality, shared with me some of her company's philosophies concerning customer service.

According to Ms. Ward-Jones, Federal Express has developed a culture that basically features a three-pronged approach:

1. They have invested the necessary dollars to create an effective system.
2. They provide 24-hour service.
3. They make two guarantees: on-time deliveries, and 30-minute written information about a shipment.

Their employees are empowered to make decisions ranging from $1,000 to $10,000, depending upon the level the employee occupies. The company puts its people (internal customers) first. An annual employee survey helps provide needed feedback to ensure that their complaints, ideas, and suggestions don't go unheeded.

Ms. Ward-Jones agrees with every other person I interviewed: the degree of success in the customer service area depends upon senior management. How does a person or a department initiate such a program? By demonstrating its effectiveness.

MISSION STATEMENT

> *Federal Express is committed to our People-Service-Profit philosophy. We will produce outstanding financial returns by providing totally reliable, competitively superior, global air-ground transportation of high priority goods and documents that require rapid, time-certain delivery.*

> *Equally important, positive control of each package will be maintained using real time electronic tracking and tracing systems. A complete record of each shipment and delivery will be presented with our request for payment. We will be helpful, courteous, and professional to each other and the public. We will strive to have a completely satisfied customer at the end of each transaction.*

My gratitude goes out to Ms. Ward-Jones for her generous sharing of time and knowledge, and to the Federal Express Corporation for being the customer-driven organization that it is.

GERBER PRODUCTS COMPANY

I had the pleasure--and I mean it was a pleasure--to speak at length with two of Gerber's key executives, Ms. Rita Van Boven, Manager of Consumer Relations, and Ms. Nancy Linder, Manager of Public Relations. Triggering the interview was, of course, the completed questionnaire I received from their company. It had all the right answers, so I simply had to find out if this company was for real. It is.

Both Ms. Van Boven and Ms. Linder (I'll refer to them as "they") were extremely generous with their time and with useful information. It was easy to tell that a true customer service culture permeates Gerber.

When asked if there was a measurable improvement in customer loyalty since the company embarked on a customer service program, they told me that ever since 1938, when Ms. Gerber began the company, there had been such a program. It seems that from the very beginning, one of the primary functions of management was to answer letters and consumers' questions.

In 1986, however, it became apparent the company could be much more effective if there was interaction between Gerber and the consumer. Consequently, they sold top management on the idea of installing an "800" number (which existed only in three states at first) so they could better, and more quickly, answer consumers' questions.

What began with 10 people receiving calls and answering questions has grown to 58 people at the present time and will grow to 75 people in 1996. (Most of them are mothers and/or grandmothers). Over 800,000 calls are received annually, the overwhelming majority of them being questions concerning every conceivable facet of taking care of babies. Customer dissatisfaction has been drastically cut and trust has grown dramatically. It's a win-win situation for both Gerber and for its customers.

Not only is Gerber able to answer a wide range of baby-related questions, but they are able to educate callers about additional products Gerber offers. In addition, the company annually sends out millions of pieces of baby-care information.

Is it easy to start such a program in your company? No, not really, unless you can sell top management on the idea. It's expensive to establish programs which interact with consumers. The alternative, however, is much less palatable.

All employees (called ambassadors) with Gerber are armed with information brochures and coupons they can distribute to anyone they encounter on the street, at meetings, or in the grocery store. Departmental boundary lines are invisible. After all, customers don't really care in which department someone works. They only know that the person with which they are talking represents the company - the receptionist, the accountant, or the CEO.

The issue of "trust" is extremely important at Gerber. Their attitude is "no one cares how much you know until they know how much you care." It was easy to tell that the people at Gerber really care.

MISSION STATEMENT

> *The primary mission of Consumer Relations is to provide superior service to all consumers. Recognizing it is they who will determine the value of our service, our intention is to exceed their expectations by sharing their concerns, responding to their needs and putting them ahead of our business procedures.*
>
> *In support of this, we are committed to:*
>
> - *Acting in a way in which customers will associate the Gerber name with quality products and service they can trust.*
> - *Increasing long term brand loyalty.*
> - *Offering a responsive, humanistic approach to problem solving.*

My gratitude goes out to Rita Van Boven and to Nancy Linder for their generosity, sincerity, and candor.

THE H. R. CHALLY GROUP

The H. R. Chally Group was founded in 1973 through a grant from the U.S. Justice Department to develop selection tests to measure the skills and motivation of police candidates and predict who would be most successful. The group's next goal was to adapt its tests to the study of salespeople and marketing environments. Since that time, it has evaluated over 100,000 sales people.

Today, The Chally Group is an internationally recognized technology leader in scientific assessment and prediction for sales selection and development testing, customer and prospect marketing strategies, and management motivation assessment.

Consequently, I thought it would be of particular interest to feature this organization for you, especially since it helps match marketing and service strategies to the added value needs which predict customer satisfaction and prospect buying. Ms. Cheryl D. Gier, Director of Sales, was my contact.

According to Ms. Gier, The Chally Group recently completed the first World Class Sales Benchmarking study. Their interviews with over 1,000 corporate customers established three major needs customers expected vendors and sellers to address:

1. Customers want to narrow their own focus to the few things they do best, and out-source

the rest without the added overhead costs of supervising their suppliers;

2. Customers want sellers to know their business well enough to create products and services they wouldn't have been able to design or create themselves; and,
3. Customers want proof that their supplier has added value in excess of price.

One of the results of the comprehensive study conducted by The Chally Group was the establishment of eight sales benchmark process areas. Guess what the first area is: establishing a customer-driven sales culture.

Even though The Chally Group is obviously at the leading edge of customer service knowledge and practices, Ms. Gier still reminded me that creating a true customer service culture cannot be done all at once. It takes time, patience, and persistence to convince your employees and your customers that your organization is "for real" when it comes to excellence in customer service.

When I asked her what the best way is to convince others in an organization to employ excellent customer service, she reiterated that the idea works best when it comes from top management. But even then, you must continue educating and pointing out your competitors' problems, especially if their customer service practices are substandard.

The Chally Group doesn't wait to take corrective action until one of its customers complains. It makes it a point to be proactive rather than reactive. Company representatives call on their "key" accounts (large customers) every three months and on their smaller customers annually to obtain ideas, suggestions, and to hear complaints.

MISSION STATEMENT

> *The purpose of The Chally customer services group is to make sure the outside customers receive single contact point service while striving to meet or exceed their needs. This will always be provided in a caring manner so that the customers enjoy doing business with and return to Chally for their future needs.*

I want to thank Ms. Cheryl Gier for sharing her organization's philosophies, for all of the supporting material she sent me, and for her candor during our interview. This is the type of organization which sets the standard for others to follow.

MARRIOTT-SAN ANTONIO RIVERCENTER

Mr. Walter Kennedy, Resident Manager of the San Antonio Marriott Rivercenter, returned one of the most nearly perfectly-answered questionnaires. The questions had been answered just as if I had prompted him.

For instance, when rating statements referring to how committed his hotel is to providing excellent customer service, and even <u>exceeding</u> customer expectations, he circled the number "5," the highest rating. That, in itself, was not all that noteworthy since almost all respondents answered similarly. However, when rating statement number 5 (Our employees are expected to follow procedures in all customer service situations), he circled the number "1," meaning "not at all." Bravo!

That's how <u>all</u> organizations should have answered statement 5, but unfortunately, few of them did. It sort of makes one wonder how an organization can say it truly exhibits excellent customer service practices, yet requires its employees to follow established procedures in all cases. It's simply not congruent. Employees must be empowered to make on-the-spot decisions and they simply cannot follow "policy" in every case.

In any event, Marriott has its act together. Included in Marriott's response was a tri-fold laminated card on which was printed their Principles of Hospitality, their Mission Statement, and their Core Values.

PRINCIPLES OF HOSPITALITY

1. Smile and greet every guest.
2. Speak to the guest in a warm, friendly, courteous manner.
3. Display genuine and enthusiastic interest in the guest.
4. Anticipate guest needs and be flexible in responding to them
5. Be knowledgeable about your job.
6. Learn to take ownership of guest problems and resolve them

MISSION STATEMENT

Our mission is to grow a worldwide lodging business using Total Quality Management principles to continuously improve preference and profitability. Our commitment is that <u>every guest leaves satisfied!</u>

CORE VALUES (PRIDE)

- Provide consistently excellent service to ensure that every guest leaves satisfied.
- Respect and care for each other because every job and every associate is important.
- Improve continuously the delivery of our products and service.
- Deliver financial success to owners and shareholders.
- Ensure we as corporate citizens are committed to bettering our community.

INTERVIEW

Mr. Walter Kennedy appeared as crisp and professional, yet personable, as do the associates who are employed at his hotel. When I asked him what advice he would give to someone trying to institute a true customer service philosophy, he simply answered, "Don't cram it down their throats. You need a 'grass roots' movement. Everybody has to buy in."

He hastened to add that not everyone will be a "believer." However, if managers remain true to their principles and beliefs, then they can create an environment to nurture their employees. The real secret? Hire friendly people. They can be trained to do what needs to be done, but it is difficult to make employees friendly, no matter how proficient they may be.

After his employees (Marriott refers to them as "associates") have been on the job for 4 to 5 weeks, he personally meets with them. One of his questions to them is, "What would you want someone to do for you if you were the customer?"

Marriott's philosophy must be working. It's difficult to argue with success.

NEGATIVE CASE STUDIES

I believe that it is appropriate to begin a new chapter with positive examples. Consequently, we began this chapter with a review of positive, personal interviews that I had with ten organizations. And I'm sure you'll agree, that they were enlightening, inspirational and encouraging.

Unfortunately, I would be remiss if I did not include a discussion of several organizations in our survey that "missed the mark," so to speak. Although they have the desire to practice excellent customer service, they simply don't yet enjoy a total customer service culture. Not that they won't, you understand. It's just that they must keep working at improving their situations and truly become obsessed with customer service, not just lip service.

Following are case studies of several organizations that simply don't measure up to the first several that we interviewed. However, sadly enough, even these are better than average.

COMPANY A

In order to graphically illustrate the negative state of customer service in this organization, its entire questionnaire is reproduced below in Figure 8-A.

Figure 8-A

		Not at all	A little	Some-what	Quite a bit	Describes it exactly
1.	Our organization is <u>totally</u> committed to providing excellent customer service.				4	
2.	Our goal is to regularly <u>exceed</u> customer expectations.			3		
3.	The quality of our product or services is measured by our customers.			3		
4.	Quality is defined as a "conformance to requirements."			3		
5.	Our employees are expected to follow procedures in all customer service situations.				4	
6.	We treat our employees as we expect them to treat our customers.			3		
7.	We regularly request feedback from our customers.		2			
8.	We utilized information from our customers to design our products and services.	1				
9.	We make it easy for customers to complain to us.			3		
10.	We educate our customers to most effectively utilize our products and services.			3		
11.	A part of each executive's job is direct customer contact.	1				
12.	Our employees at various levels meet directly with customers.		2			

13.	All employees are expected to do what it takes to meet or exceed customer expectations.	1				
14.	Employees are recognized and/or rewarded for "bending the rules" to meet a customer's need.	1				
15.	All employees are routinely educated about our products and services.		2			
16.	All levels of employees have a say in how their job is performed and measured.		2			
17.	Our employees are cross-trained so that they fill in for each other.			3		
18.	Employees do what it takes to help a customer even if it "isn't their job."		2			
19.	The first criteria for promotion is customer service, whether internal or external customers.			3		
20.	Continuing self development, college, or professional designation courses are encouraged.		2			
21.	Self development is supported with financial aid.				4	
22.	Self development must be outside of normal work hours.					5
23.	Departmental boundaries are intentionally invisible to the customer.		2			
24.	Teamwork is rewarded above individual accomplishment.			3		
25.	Our organization department heads work together to eliminate mistakes and defects before they occur.	1				

Note that there is only one 5 circled on the entire questionnaire. Particularly note the 1's and the 2's on statements 7, 8, 11 through 16, 18, 20, 23, and 25. The only 5 rating was on statement 22 (Self development must be outside of normal work hours). Ouch!

To cap it all off, when asked for a copy of their mission statement, their answer was, "We are in the process of changing our mission statement and I do not have it available at this time." This company is a large, nationally recognized organization - unfortunately without direction.

COMPANY B

A question frequently raised in my seminars is "Why should monopolies or governmental agencies be concerned with providing excellent customer service? After all, they're the only game in town, so why worry?"

Well, things are changing. Governmental agencies are beginning to feel the effects of irate taxpayers. They are asking questions such as: "Could a private entity perform the job better and at a lower cost?" The answer in many cases is yes. Company B faces just such a dilemma.

When asked what the greatest problem Company B faced, the answer was an "increased competition into our previous monopoly." Oooooh! Monopolies and arrogant governmental workers take note. Maybe you can save your job by changing your attitudes.

Company B seems to have its share of problems. Note how many 1's and 2's it has: 6, 11 through 19, 22, 23, and 25. At least they were honest and also rated themselves low on statement 1. Unfortunately, it went down hill from there.

Figure 8-B

		Not at all	A little	Some-what	Quite a bit	Describes it exactly
1.	Our organization is <u>totally</u> committed to providing excellent customer service.			3		
2.	Our goal is to regularly <u>exceed</u> customer expectations.				4	
3.	The quality of our product or services is measured by our customers.			3		
4.	Quality is defined as a "conformance to requirements."				4	
5.	Our employees are expected to follow procedures in all customer service situations.			3		
6.	We treat our employees as we expect them to treat our customers.	1				
7.	We regularly request feedback from our customers.				4	
8.	We utilized information from our customers to design our products and services.			3		
9.	We make it easy for customers to complain to us.			3		
10.	We educate our customers to most effectively utilize our products and services.				4	
11.	A part of each executive's job is direct customer contact.	1				
12.	Our employees at various levels meet directly with customers.		2			

13.	All employees are expected to do what it takes to meet or exceed customer expectations.		2	
14.	Employees are recognized and/or rewarded for "bending the rules" to meet a customer's need.		2	
15.	All employees are routinely educated about our products and services.		2	
16.	All levels of employees have a say in how their job is performed and measured.		2	
17.	Our employees are cross-trained so that they fill in for each other.	1		
18.	Employees do what it takes to help a customer even if it "isn't their job."		2	
19.	The first criteria for promotion is customer service, whether internal or external customers.		2	
20.	Continuing self development, college, or professional designation courses are encouraged.			3
21.	Self development is supported with financial aid.			3
22.	Self development must be outside of normal work hours.		2	
23.	Departmental boundaries are intentionally invisible to the customer.	1		
24.	Teamwork is rewarded above individual accomplishment.			3
25.	Our organization department heads work together to eliminate mistakes and defects before they occur.		2	

COMPANY C

Well, just when you thought it couldn't get any worse, it did. The next organization obviously is suffering from severe internal problems and won't be able to improve its customer service attitude until it cleans up its internal mess.

As in the previous examples, I have reprinted their entire questionnaire (Figure 8-C), so you can see for yourself the sad state of affairs this company is enduring.

Figure 8-C

		Not at all	A little	Some-what	Quite a bit	Describes it exactly
1.	Our organization is totally committed to providing excellent customer service.			3		
2.	Our goal is to regularly exceed customer expectations.	1				
3.	The quality of our product or services is measured by our customers.		2			
4.	Quality is defined as a "conformance to requirements."			3		
5.	Our employees are expected to follow procedures in all customer service situations.			3		
6.	We treat our employees as we expect them to treat our customers.	1				
7.	We regularly request feedback from our customers.				4	
8.	We utilized information from our customers to design our products and services.	1				
9.	We make it easy for customers to complain to us.			3		
10.	We educate our customers to most effectively utilize our products and services.				4	
11.	A part of each executive's job is direct customer contact.			3		
12.	Our employees at various levels meet directly with customers.		2			

13.	All employees are expected to do what it takes to meet or exceed customer expectations.		2			
14.	Employees are recognized and/or rewarded for "bending the rules" to meet a customer's need.		2			
15.	All employees are routinely educated about our products and services.		2			
16.	All levels of employees have a say in how their job is performed and measured.	1				
17.	Our employees are cross-trained so that they fill in for each other.		2			
18.	Employees do what it takes to help a customer even if it "isn't their job."		2			
19.	The first criteria for promotion is customer service, whether internal or external customers.	1				
20.	Continuing self development, college, or professional designation courses are encouraged.	1				
21.	Self development is supported with financial aid.	1				
22.	Self development must be outside of normal work hours.				4	
23.	Departmental boundaries are intentionally invisible to the customer.	1				
24.	Teamwork is rewarded above individual accomplishment.	1				
25.	Our organization department heads work together to eliminate mistakes and defects before they occur.		2			

Note the 1's and 2's on statements 2,3,6,8,12 through 18, 19 through 21, and 23 through 25.

When asked to specifically list their greatest problems, their reply was as follows:

1. Lack of flexibility to change directions or make decisions to meet market wants and needs.
2. Top-down control of management style.
3. No long-term focus or planning.
4. Barriers between departments (turf protection).
5. Lack of continuous improvement process.

How long do you thing this will survive? It's doing everything wrong. Real customer service is not even in its vocabulary. However, I am most grateful for the honest answers and sincerely hope that the person who filled out my questionnaire will be able to effect some positive changes - quickly.

9 EDUCATORS NEED EDUCATION TOO!

"Everything has changed but our ways of thinking, and if these do not change we drift toward unparalleled catastrophe."–**Albert Einstein**

A WHOLE NEW BALL GAME

Remember the days when only a small percentage of graduating high school seniors were college bound? It was considered a real privilege to attend the college or university of your choice. After all, only such professionals as doctors, dentists, and lawyers really needed to learn all those facts and figures in order properly to perform their work.

Today, the necessity of having a college degree is as great as having a high school diploma was only a few years ago. Consequently, an increasing number of students have been entering colleges and universities. So many, in fact, that many institutions of higher learning have adopted a snobby attitude.

After all, why be concerned with every student? There were plenty of other students available, so why worry if a few became unhappy or flunked out?

Well, things are changing, and I have to admit that I wasn't aware of these changes until a few years ago. It all began when I received an invitation to present an all-day customer service seminar at The University of Texas at San Antonio. While it is true that I had presented such seminars and workshops for corporations, I had never considered doing so for a school.

I began researching this newfound facet and quickly discovered several major universities had begun to realize the obvious--students are their customers. Wow! What a revelation!

AN AMERICAN IMPERATIVE: HIGHER EXPECTATIONS FOR HIGHER EDUCATION

In an open letter to those concerned with the American future from the Wingspread Group on Higher Education, the consensus is that there is a dangerous mismatch between what American society needs from higher education and what it is receiving. In other words, our colleges and universities are not generally providing excellent service to their customers (students).

The Wingspread Report goes on to say, "Like much of the rest of American education, the nations' colleges and universities appear to live by an unconscious educational rule of thumb that their function is to weed out, not to cultivate, students for whom they have accepted responsibility. An unacceptably high percentage of students leaks out of the system at each juncture in the education pipeline."

I believe this situation exists especially in large state universities. My wife, older daughter, and I each attended large universities and were generally given the same individual consideration as a rancher would give a herd of cattle. On the other hand, our younger daughter attended a small private college where the situation was entirely different.

There, students are treated with respect and are personally challenged to be all that they can be. They are not just a number; they have a name.

Unfortunately, it is these very schools which face the biggest recruiting problems, partly because of the cost of attending such an institution. Ironically, in our case at least, our costs for sending our daughter to a small, expensive, private school was similar to the cost of sending our older daughter to a large state university. Why? Because the smaller institution cared enough to help us obtain financial aid, whereas the large state university didn't exert any effort at all to help.

To make matters even worse, too many institutions fail to prepare their students to compete in the global economy. It is true that some entrants are ill-prepared, some institutions have severe cost problems, and some students simply don't want to learn anything except how to spend their parents' money. However, the Wingspread Report continues, " the simple fact is that some faculties and institutions certify for graduation too many students who cannot read and write very well, too many whose intellectual depth and breadth are unimpressive, and too many whose skills are inadequate in the face of the demands of contemporary life." What an indictment!

According to the 1993 National Adult Literacy Survey (NALS), as mentioned in An American Imperative: Higher Expectations for Higher Education, a large number of college graduates are unable, in everyday situations, to use basic skills involving reading, writing, computation, and elementary problem-solving. As a matter of fact, only about one-half of four-year graduates are able to demonstrate intermediate levels of competence in the areas of working with documents, with prose, and with quantitative skills.

WHAT SHOULD WE BE GETTING?

As reported by The Wall Street Journal on February 21, 1995, ("Employers Give Schools Low Grade on Job Preparation"), employers have a dismal view of the ways schools and universities prepare people for the workplace. The Wall Street Journal reported that, "A survey of 3,347 companies, made by the Census Bureau for the Education Department, shows managers estimate that one out of every five U.S. employees isn't proficient in the job. There is a 'disconnection' between the U.S. school system and employers."

According to An American Imperative, our society needs stronger, more vital forms of community. It needs an informed and involved citizenry. It needs graduates able to assume leadership roles in American life. It needs a competent and adaptable work force. It needs an affordable, cost-effective educational enterprise offering lifelong learning. Above all, it needs a commitment to the American promise--the idea that all Americans have the opportunity to develop their talents to the fullest.

The elite are becoming educated, no doubt. Our graduate and professional schools are doing a credible job of preparing scientists, engineers, and other professionals, but they represent only about the top 20 percent of the population. What we need, of course, in order to remain competitive in a global economy, is to train the remaining 80 percent of the population in basic reading, writing, computational, information processing, teamwork, and learning skills which will allow them to adapt to new technology and knowledge.

Easy to say, right? How do we do it? The nation's colleges and universities must focus overwhelmingly on what their students learn and achieve. Again, according to An American Imperative, "We must redesign all of our learning systems to align our entire education enterprise with the personal, civic, and work place needs of this century. Finally, students and parents should look to the value added to their lives, not simply to the prestige of the institutions they attend."

In summary, our colleges and universities must begin to exercise excellence in customer service by giving students their money's worth. Professors must stop tripping over their egos, and begin caring about each and every one of their students--cultivate them, not cull them.

The administration must realize before it's too late that it has many customers--its students, their parents, alumni, townspeople, visitors, civic groups, high schoolers, and public.

This is a wake-up call for all 3,400 campuses serving over 12 million students in this nation. Treat your students as if they make a difference, because they do. They're your customers.

SLUGGING IT OUT

Some institutions are seeing the light. According to The Wall Street Journal's April 6, 1994 issue, there is a royal battle going on between our nations' graduate business schools. It seems the number of MBA prospects taking the Graduate Management Admissions Test has dropped 17% since 1991. Charles Hickman, director of projects and services for the American Assembly of Collegiate Schools of Business says, "Business schools in general are getting squeezed these days, and mid-level schools are feeling it most."

As competition for students heats up, top-ranked schools are poaching on their lesser-known counterparts. According to Hickman, compounding the problem are continuing cutbacks in traditional markets for MBA's. Large companies are cutting middle management positions and are offering less tuition support for their employees.

I don't mean to imply that top-tier business graduate schools such as The University of Texas at Austin, Harvard, or Stanford will be running out of students any time soon. However, numerous mid-tier schools are already changing their ways of doing business.

For instance, The University of Denver's business school is choosing women as its niche. Seattle University is no longer merely waiting for students to come to it; it is taking the school to them by teaching evening and breakfast MBA courses in rented office space near Seattle's largest employers. Fordham University and Loyola offer MBA courses in Deming's "Total Quality Management," according to The Wall Street Journal.

In other words, institutions of higher learning are beginning to wake up and are reading the trend. Just as in any other business, simply opening up your doors doesn't necessarily mean customers will flock to you.

PRIMARY AND SECONDARY SCHOOLS

Some of the more progressive and forward-thinking colleges and universities are grabbing the bull by the horns and adapting their attitudes to include the necessity of exhibiting excellence in customer service. But what about our primary and secondary schools?

My wife is a middle school teacher. While she is dedicated to the idea of expanding her students' knowledge, much of her time is wasted by fulfilling state and national paperwork requirements. Unruly students' actions must be carefully documented in order to effect a reprimand, suspension, or expulsion. In fact, there is so much red tape involved, sometimes it simply isn't worth the effort to pursue disciplining offending students.

Students should come to school ready to learn. They should come to school with some respect for rules and regulations. They should come to school and act like human beings instead of like zombies. Some do; many don't.

While it is true that students are the schools' customers, teachers are too. Yet, in many cases, they are treated like second class citizens, work long hours, and receive minimal recognition.

George W. Bush, Jr., the new Governor of Texas, has pledged a new emphasis on education in the state. He favors local control, instead of centralized control in Austin. It's about time to take schools back from those who have made them almost impossible to function because of all the bureaucratic red tape.

Let teachers teach; let students learn; and leave the lawyers out.

STUDENTS ARE PEOPLE TOO

A whole new movement is sweeping this country with regard to education. No longer is it enough to be top-heavy with tenured professors who are more interested in promoting their own images than in developing their students' minds. No longer is it acceptable to run local schools from afar with strange and alien concepts. No longer is permissible to operate with a smug attitude.

It's high time public schools adopt a similar attitude to that of private schools. There, parents have a "hammer." If the administration, or the teachers, don't care enough to exhibit a real caring attitude, parents can simply yank their children out of school. Or if the school fails to espouse parents' values and desires, the child can be removed.

In short, in order for private schools to continue existing, they must demonstrate excellence in customer service. If they don't, they die.

There are more of you reading this book who are students or parents than are school administrators. So how does this new theory help you?

You now have permission to stand up for your rights. It's your money. It's your life. You don't have to put up with their lousy service any longer.

Demand service. Demand to be recognized. Demand to get your money's worth.

If they won't comply, go some other place if you can, or go as high up the line as you need in order to change the attitudes.

DON'T LET 'EM FORGET WHO'S THE BOSS. EDUCATE 'EM!

WHAT ABOUT THE LITTLE PEOPLE?

There exists a national group called "Success by 6" which believes the most important education children receive must happen years before they begin school. They, like many others, believe education should start in the womb and continue right up to the first day of kindergarten.

Studies have shown that children learn more and develop faster during their first five years of their lives than at any other time in their lives. This is the time during which they learn to use motor skills, conceive ideas, and develop language skills, as well as develop trust and a sense of autonomy.

The problem is most education historically hasn't begun until the child enters school. By then it's almost too late. So we end up with an increase in violent crimes, more prisons, and a poorly prepared work force.

The problem doesn't stop there, however. Once children do enter school, many parents continue shunning their responsibilities. Their excuses are creative, but fall on deaf ears. Figure 9-1 illustrates reasons why parents don't get involved in their children's' education.

Figure 9-1

Why Parents Don't Get Involved

Do not have enough time	89%
Feel they have nothing to contribute	32%
Don't understand the system to know how to be involved	32%
Lack of child care	28%
Feel intimidated	25%
Can't attend PTA/school functions at times scheduled	18%
Language and cultural differences	15%
Don't have access to transportation to attend functions	11%
Do not feel welcome at the school	9%

Source: San Antonio Express-News, Feb. 7, 1995.

SUMMARY

Well, we have covered the gamut--colleges, primary and secondary education, and the little folks. The fact is: someone at each level should be responsible for educating the populace. Let's each meet the challenge and do our parts. Time and money spent now will save untold millions later.

"We cannot ask Americans to be better citizens if we are not better servants."– President Bill Clinton, in his State of the Union address, January 24, 1995.

I have been looking forward to writing this chapter, because I believe that if any entity should practice excellence in customer service, it should be our government. Unfortunately, however, many people employed by our government and who are paid by our tax dollars have forgotten what their purpose should be. It is because of this fact that the public revolted in 1994 and threw out the Democratic majority in Congress and screamed for change.

Government and its agents should exist to serve those who elected it. When it stops doing so, we must demand that it change and live up to its purpose.

GOVERNMENT HAS FORGOTTEN ITS CLIENTS

Columnist Don Feder recently reminded us that "Americans, who had forgotten the nature of the liberal contagion during the cozy Reagan years, got an ice-cold shower without a towel over the past 21 months."

He went on to say, "Americans are fed up with taxes, outraged over crime, and alienated by illegal immigration, as can be seen in the landslide victory of California's Proposition 187. Sixty-nine percent of the American people say the nation is heading in the wrong direction."

I agree. A government, whose most notable achievements include appointing a surgeon general who pushed condoms and considered drug legalization, judges who are soft on criminals, a Justice Department which tried to weaken child pornography laws, a Congress which supported the protection of obscure species at the expense of people and allowing leeches in our society to drain the resources of the working people, must be discarded.

Let me remind you of how poor our government's customer service has become by citing several examples.

The Energy Department

"So What Do People At Energy Department Do All Day Long?" read the headlines in the December 15, 1994 issue of The Wall Street Journal. Evidently, not much; at least not much that is useful to you and me.

According to The Journal, the Department of Energy was targeted for elimination altogether, although it will now probably be spared with a 20% budget cut. Senate Majority Leader, Bob Dole states, "I don't see any useful purpose it serves."

One mid-level Department of Energy official explained, "We probably spend half our time doing very routine, almost administrative things, like answering mail." They also attend meetings in other offices within the agency "on programs over which we have broad oversight but not a lot of responsibility."

"Still," The Journal continues, "the lawyers toil on." About 40 of them spend their days pursuing oil companies who violated federal price regulations, even though the rules were eliminated 13 years ago. Even the lawyer who originated most of the subject lawsuits, but who is now in private practice, admits that the pursuit of these cases is "almost a legal archaeology program after all these years. You have to ask how sensible a deployment of investment of federal resources it is."

Who do you think is paying for all this make-work?

Judson Independent School District

On November 19, 1994, the San Antonio Judson ISD passed a $45 million bond package by a 68 percent to 32 percent margin. The Justice Department, in all of its wisdom, however, ruled the election invalid because Judson hadn't provided Spanish-speaking voters with adequate information about the proposal.

The truth is, however, only 2,000 Hispanics (about 3 percent) in the district allegedly needed such assistance--hardly enough to overturn the election even if every one of them had voted against the proposal. Superintendent Galen Elolf's view is that the Justice Department's decision was completely arbitrary. (Could it be that the employees in the Justice Department didn't have enough to do?).

As you might have guessed by now, a new election was held in January, 1995. The results? Judson School District voters overwhelmingly approved the $45 million bond issue for the second time. Except this time it counted.

Remember, back in November, voters approved the bond issue by slightly more than 2-to-1. This time, they approved it 1,766 for and 841 against - again by more than 2-to-1!

Mr. Tony Garza, the resident (and a perennial politician who never wins anything) who filed the complaint against the district in the first place, remarked that he was glad the district was abiding by the law and he had no regrets about the extra money spent.

Wow! Isn't it great spending other people's money? Oh, incidentally, his group displayed only one flyer opposing the bond issue--ENTIRELY IN ENGLISH. Just another case of more time and more money wasted, more governmental interference--and less customer service.

Wouldn't it have been great if the Justice Department had kept its nose out of Judson's affairs? It would have saved taxpayers a substantial amount of money and avoided providing a gross disservice.

Proposition 187

California voters spoke loudly and clearly. They, like the vast majority of Americans, are gagging on the incredibly unfair tax-gobbling antics which are being forced down their throats. The point is: our government is forcing the American public to pay for the general welfare of illegal immigrants and their offspring.

Proposition 187, approved by 59 percent of California voters in November, 1994 would have denied health and social services, as well as public schooling to illegal immigrants. However, U.S. District Judge Mariana Phaelzer granted a preliminary injunction blocking almost all of Proposition 187's bans.

The question this kind of action raises is, "when is our government going to begin providing customer service to its clients--the vast majority of Americans?"

Texas Has a Similar Problem

The State of Texas has a similar problem to that of California concerning illegal aliens. Recently, however, U.S. District Judge Filemon Vela indicated he will probably dismiss Texas' lawsuit which demands that the federal government foot the billion-dollar bill for Texas' providing services to its illegal immigrants. Florida and other states with large illegal alien populations have filed similar suits.

In a feeble attempt at appeasement, Congress has authorized $1.8 billion over six years to reimburse states which have large populations of illegal immigrants for their criminal justice costs. Well, Texas' cost alone is $1.3 billion per year. Once again, the federal government is failing miserably at providing excellence in customer service to the very people whom it should be serving. It seems to be more interested in being "politically correct" and walking on eggs so as not to offend certain minority groups.

San Antonio's Aquifer

San Antonio receives its drinking water from an underground source, called the Edwards Aquifer. Water from rainfall as far away as 150 miles to the west seeps into vast limestone formations, travels underground in an easterly direction, and eventually finds its way to hundreds of water wells. The City of San Antonio is the largest city in the country to receive all of its water from such an underground source. Efforts are ongoing to prevent the pollution of the Edwards Aquifer, and most residents understand and appreciate the importance of maintaining this clean source of water.

Eventually, after seeping for a couple of hundred of miles, water that has not been tapped bubbles out of the ground at the Comal Springs in New Braunfels and at San Marcos, two small towns 30 miles northeast of San Antonio. For years, farmers and ranchers in the Central Texas area have tapped into this natural resource for drinking and irrigation purposes. And that is where the rub comes in.

Little Crawly Things

It seems there exists within these springs at New Braunfels several insignificant species which happen to appear on the sacred "Endangered Species" list. The Sierra Club has filed suit to limit pumping of the Edwards Aquifer so as to ensure an adequate spring flow for the species--even to the detriment of a million or so people who reside in the greater San Antonio area.

The irony of the entire matter is that during 1951-1957, Central Texas experienced a severe drought and the springs ceased flowing during that time. The subject species, which later appeared on the "Endangered Species" list, all survived quite well, thank you, by simply wiggling their way through the rock crevices until they found adequate water.

One would surmise they could once again do the same in the event the springs stop flowing. Or they could be dipped out of the springs and be held in holding tanks until the springs begin flowing again, or they could be transferred to other similar springs across the country. To further add insult to injury, most of these species aren't even indigenous to the area. They were introduced, not by nature, but by humans--so they had to come from somewhere else, right?

Simply stated, this whole issue has become a political football. Even San Antonio's former mayor, Nelson Wolff, called the terms given to San Antonio by the EPA an abuse of federal power.

Now there sits out in Midland, Texas, which is several hundreds of miles away, Senior U.S. District Judge Lucius D. Bunton III who is someday going to rule on the Sierra Club's suit. Will he help the federal government administer customer service to the millions who need water to live, work, and play; or will he follow the all-too-familiar pattern of our government's "the people be damned" attitude? Only time will tell. Any bets?

Private Property

To further illustrate how our government is trying to pillage its customers (especially property owners), the following articles are included. They succinctly identify the rampant, deceitful actions our government is perpetrating upon us:

"Too much worry over waning of some species"–T. R. Fehrenbach, San Antonio Express-News, January 22, 1995. (Reprinted with permission).

Society suffers from many man-made plagues, and the Endangered Species Act of 1973 is one of them.

This act was, of course, well-meaning. It was inspired primarily by the plight of the bald eagle, our national emblem, which was threatened with extinction in the lower 48 states by loss of habitat, hunting, and pollution. The peregrine falcon was another admirable species near the point of vanishing. The act was designed to save them.

But, as Congress so often does in fits of inattention, the legislation was left open-ended and handed over to bureaucrats to regulate. From three or four "endangered species" soon numbered in the hundreds, and some were exotic indeed - nobody ever heard of them.

The snail darters, spotted owls, and boat-tailed rats were bound to be discovered, since finding more “threatened” species and saving them is the bureaucrats' bread, butter, and promotion ladder. To save many such critters, their habitats must be preserved and undisturbed by human hands- and this is where the raging controversies erupted.

Readers no doubt are aware of the horror stories from coast to coast: jobs lost in the timber industry; homes destroyed by fire because brush may not be cut; and last, but hardly least, San Antonio's dilemma with obscure aquatic life and water levels.

You may not know that in some places cedar may not be cleared in the Hill Country, and most Texas ranchers would like to play feds and farmers, in the sense that our forefathers acted out cowboys and Indians.

The problem is, if you own property and if an ocelot or jaguarundi is found on it, unless you shoot and bury it by the dark of the moon, in effect you may no longer own your property. The species does, by federal fiat. You may fell no tree, cut no brush, build no house, draw no water, lest endangered life be disturbed. Because of some forms of life or another, sometimes even microscopic, this policy is a threat to dozens of counties. Now this is a form of environmentalism run amok.

Though courts have found otherwise, it runs counter to the ethos of a private-right-protecting capitalist society, and also the Constitution, which sets forth that no governmental agency may "take" private property without due compensation.

Indeed, everything has a price, and if the public wants to freeze endangered species' habitats from further development and use, well and good - but let the public pay for it, just as it pays for property gobbled up by roads and public rights-of-way.

Lately, the Supreme Court has started to look askance at lower courts' decisions holding that "restrictions" upon use are not "takings." The better news is that Congress is likely to legislate this sooner. Courts heed lawyers; Congress has a broader constituency.

Otherwise, groups such as tree huggers and lumberjacks, Sierra Club honchos and San Antonians, may indulge in a bit of intra-species extermination.

This tendency toward reason, however, raises panic among extreme "environmentalists," who sense the American public simply will not cough up millions to save some form of shrimp life. So be prepared for tantrums and fits of raw emotionalism interspersed with the interconnectedness-of-all-life notions set forth as science.

There is, of course, no question that many forms of life are threatened across the world, mostly by man's alterations of the environment. Some species disappear each year. But trying to block this completely is neither good public policy nor science. Some species can be saved, some cannot. We should try, I think, to preserve bald eagles, birds, and mammals of which we're fond, or species which, like gray wolves, perform an ecological function. And we should be prepared to pay for such preservation.

However, species have been vanishing for millions of years, most of them long before our own got here. Ask a geologist where oil or gas comes from, or a paleontologist about dinosaur bones. We have, in fact, identified thousands of life forms which once lived upon the earth and long since have become extinct.

True environmentalists know there is no "balance of nature" but rather an unstable state, constantly shifting. Every living species must adapt to constant change or perish, whether this is wrought by man or comet-fall.

The universe has its own survival mechanism, operated through the transmittal of genes. Nature's God seems to regard individual extinction with equanimity. The world outlives most things, just as it may well outlast us.

And that's the rub: Our own self-absorbed species does not care to contemplate this, and it sees its own fate in all vanishing forms of life. We would play Canute.

For many Americans, preventing extinction has become an obsession. Too many think that every falling leaf presages our cosmic fate and want to stop the fall. Many are sincere in this emotion, but many have other agendas entirely.

Ruffle many virulent "environmentalist's" feathers, and anti-capitalist, anti-private-property, and anti-technological-society rhetoric spews out. For these folks, the world is flat and no evidence will convince them otherwise.

However, in due time, they also may become extinct.

"What's the Cost? Private Property, Public Use"--Dr. Charles E. Gilliland, Associate Research Economist, Texas A&M University (Reprinted with permission).

The implementation of various environmental laws, but most notably the Endangered Species Act, has created a confrontation between property owners on one side and environmentalists and government agencies on the other. This dispute centers on rival concepts of the basic nature of private property rights that ultimately focuses on the methods used to finance environmental preservation. The traditional view of private property is founded on the belief that individuals have a right to gain the fruits of their labors. By combining their industry with land, individuals create wealth and thus are inherently justified in claiming exclusive rights to the property they own.

Responding to this belief, the founding fathers incorporated protection for private property in the Bill of Rights by barring government's taking private property for public purposes without compensating the owners. The goal is to leave a property owner economically whole when a public taking becomes necessary and to have the public share the cost of a public project.

Protected by this Fifth Amendment guarantee, owners have the incentive to pursue the wisest use of their property guided by the preferences and mores of society. Personal gain from increasing values leads owners to produce the goods that are in demand. As a result, property owners generally conserve and care for their property rather than exploit or destroy it recklessly. Without these guarantees, individuals have few incentives to conserve resources.

Two centuries of American development have institutionalized the eminent domain process to provide just compensation for public takings of private property. When roads, dams, floodways and other public projects require private property, owners receive monetary or in-kind settlements that reflect the market value of their properties prior to the taking. Creation of national wildlife refuges on private lands resulted in compensation to owners. As national parks and national forests expanded, owners were compensated with cash or land. Although owners sometimes felt short-changed, the eminent domain process has served well to transfer property to public projects while leaving the previous owners economically intact.

Providing for preservation of endangered species and wetlands appears to fit this time-honored tradition. In creating the Aransas Wildlife Refuge that serves as home to the whooping crane, for example, the government purchased and permanently set aside an area for the endangered species. This process left private property owners' wealth unchanged and provided a home for the threatened creatures. Similar preserves could be acquired for more recently identified endangered species.

Alternative Perspective

For several reasons, proponents of environmental preservation reject the idea of compensating owners for losses resulting from regulations. The Endangered Species Act regards all threatened creatures as deserving equal protection. Species such as the pacific yew may hold secrets for treating cancer and provide valuable service to countless generations. Accumulating these benefits indicates an enormous value for such a specie. Because no one knows which specie harbors this kind of potential use, all species, including non-descript beetles, blind salamanders, prairie chickens and pandas, are equal under the act. Thus, the benefit of salvaging each endangered specie is assumed to be infinite.

Since the act was adopted, the number of species classified as endangered have multiplied. Currently, the U.S. Fish and Wildlife Service lists 632 endangered species in the United States (January 1994). The public budget simply cannot stretch far enough to purchase a home for them all. Requiring compensation to property owners would necessitate choosing which species can be preserved within budget constraints. Current law, however, does not contain a mechanism for making such choices.

Another view of property rights eliminates the need to compensate current owners for restrictions of property uses. Under this doctrine, nonowners have a stake in the way owners manage properties; current owners then are stewards temporarily entrusted with the property to preserve it for the public and for future generations. From this perspective, property is not a justified claim but rather an entitlement granted to individuals by the public stakeholders.

Property ownership then becomes similar to a driver's license, which can be revoked or modified at any time. Owners--or licensees--can pursue only those activities that have been approved by the licensing authority. In other words, any land use not previously approved by the government conceivably could be prohibited unless the government first grants permission. Government could even bar previously allowed uses as societal values change.

These differing views have collided as agencies have fashioned regulations to accomplish the objectives of various environmental laws. For example, the Endangered Species Act makes it a crime to "take" an endangered creature, be it bald eagle or beetle. The act further defines take to include harassment of the creature in question, and the U.S. Fish and Wildlife Service has extended the law to cover modification of habitat even when the endangered creatures are not present. These actions have forbidden many previous property management practices such as removing cedar, building fences or even driving a tractor near the endangered animals.

The celebrated cases of the spotted owl in the Northwest and red-cockaded woodpecker in the South illustrate the effects of this kind of regulation. In another widely known case, the act precluded California homeowners from plowing firebreaks around homes near Los Angeles because the area contained habitat for an endangered kangaroo rat. As a result, several homes that could have escaped destruction burned to the ground when wildfires swept through southern California. Similar cases have been documented throughout Texas and the nation. Property rights advocates believe that such regulations restrict entire areas of privately owned land to use as an endangered species habitat. Advocates of the alternate view believe the regulations simply preserve endangered resources without changing property rights.

To Take or Not To Take

Many landowners and property rights advocates view these regulations as a serious abrogation of their property rights. They reason that such regulations clearly preclude or severely restrict profitable uses of their land and, in effect, take their property without just compensation. They retain the obligations of property owners but no longer reap the benefits. Few, if any, potential buyers want property with such restrictions in place. Because of this decrease in demand, the market value of their holdings has markedly diminished. The regulations have provided a good to society, namely preservation of endangered species, while imposing the cost on selected property owners.

Advocates of the entitlement view of property insist that a "taking" has not occurred. Rather, they believe, the actions instituting the regulations reflect a change in social values that places a premium on preserving the rapidly diminishing biodiversity of the earth. Under this system, owners can still use their property as they choose if the use does not transgress these new societal norms. Property owners have not lost the right to use their property in another fashion, these advocates contend, because they never really had that right in the first place. This kind of regulation is similar to the adoption of zoning without grandfathering; the regulations are simply adjusting behavior to the new social climate. This view holds that compensation should not be required.

The new societal norms reflected by this view see private habitat modification as an enormous cost to this and succeeding generations. By prohibiting any modification, the government keeps current owners from imposing those costs. From this perspective, the action is much like barring landowners from dumping pollutants on others.

On the other hand, private owners of land with endangered species habitat have managed their property in a manner that has sustained habitat. Because there has been no mechanism to pay them for that activity, these owners have provided this benefit to society without compensation.

Although this struggle appears to affect only selected property owners, the outcome has broad implications. First, restricting property use may cause values to fall. Second, if owners are not compensated for declines, their net worth will fall, reducing their ability to participate in economic activity. Even with reimbursement, the value of property-based assets will decline. Lenders have begun to express concern about this potential new source of risk. Because of the prospect of value losses, lenders may reject these properties as security for loans, leading to reduced borrowing power among property owners. Third, declining values on affected properties may reduce tax bases and force local taxing jurisdictions to raise tax revenues from the remaining pool of value. And finally, government actions that seem to so readily restrict control of property because of endangered species lessens the certainty of everyone's property rights.

THE CONSTITUTION

Thought for the day: If you have ever wondered just how much authority our government really has, review the Constitution--especially the Bill of Rights. In effect, it has none, except those specifically given it by the Constitution. Amendment 10 states: "The powers not delegated to the United States by the Constitution, nor prohibited by it to the States, are reserved to the States respectively, or to the people."

DISABLED ADDICTS AND ALCOHOLICS

According to a report released by the Department of Health and Human Services, over 80,000 drug addicts and alcoholics receive "disability" checks from our Santa Claus government. The average recipient has been receiving checks (currently they average $466 per month) for over seven years - some for as long as 20 years.

NEW YORK

It's not only the federal government that has done a disservice to its populace. City and state governments have done their share too.

Take the case of New York City. The March 30, 1995, issue of The Wall Street Journal reported that New York's flourishing economy of 1950 showed 3.1 million private-sector jobs. But in the 1960's, government, along with corresponding taxes, soared. By 1977, the number of private-sector jobs had plummeted to a mere 2.7 million--where it still languishes today.

Not only that, but 102 of New York's 131 Fortune 500 corporate headquarters fled, taking 500,000 jobs with them.

The more serious problem created by government welfare, however, is a social one. We have convinced the poor that they are victims of uncontrollable economic forces, or of racism that relegates them to exclusion. It's no wonder they drop out of school or fail to achieve in the workplace.

To make matters even worse, they have learned to believe that there's nothing wrong with having out-of-wedlock babies they can't support while deserving an income to do so. This grotesque phenomenon has helped dysfunctional single-parent families proliferate, passing failure from one generation to another.

-------- BUT --------

GOVERNMENT IS GETTING THE MESSAGE

On Thursday, November 10, 1994, newspaper headlines across America shouted: "Clinton to voters: I got the message." (We certainly hope so).

Again quoting: "President Clinton, stunned by a Republican revolution in midterm elections, accepted some blame Wednesday and promised to move toward the center of the political debate. He offered a tortured, often rambling, explanation for his party's whipping and challenged the incoming Republican majority in Congress to help him govern."

The fact is, the general populace has had it with "politics as usual." Voters want fundamental change in the role of government in their lives. The voters want the government that they elect to serve them--not the other way around. The voters, in short, want their government to stop portraying arrogance as it has for too many years and to begin exhibiting excellence in customer service.

As a result of the November 1994 elections, President Clinton not only "got the message," but he actually tried to move toward the political center. For instance, in the bidding war for middle-class support, he proposed a $60 billion mix of tax cuts to help families bear the cost of raising and educating their children.

Already, as early as January, 1995, racial and gender set-aside programs appeared vulnerable. Even the hallowed affirmative action programs seemed to be in trouble. The irony of affirmative action is that many minorities oppose the affirmative action concept due to the fact that such policies do little for the poor, and in fact call into question legitimate minority achievements.

In my opinion, it is poor customer service on the part of government when it becomes a modern-day Robin Hood - taking from those who earn it and giving it to those who don't. Welfare is an insidious system in which the more you spend, the more clientele you generate for the programs you create. There is no way for the country to spend its way out of poverty. Wealth redistribution does not equalize peoples. It destroys wealth. It would never work in the business world and it doesn't work in the political world either.

I'm certain that the next several years will witness continuing struggles between Democrats and Republicans, liberals and conservatives, to determine who will eventually win. Let me provide some insight to those who are serious about winning: The political party or the philosophical conviction that will prevail is the one which provides true excellence in customer service to the American public.

11 KIDS ARE PEOPLE TOO!

It has been an exciting and fulfilling experience for me to be able to speak to junior high and senior high school students all over the state of Texas. And from what I've observed, I believe our future is in good hands.

Two of the organizations I have addressed are the FHA/HERO (Future Homemakers of America/Home Economic Related Occupations) and the BPA (Business Professionals of America). These outstanding young people come from all kinds of environments, but they all have one thing in common--they want to succeed in life.

Unfortunately, however, not all young people share this vision. How do we know that?

Well, one out of ten are hooked on marijuana; there are 3 million teenage alcoholics in this country (every 15 seconds one of them is involved in a car wreck and every 23 minutes one of them dies as a result); there will be one million teenage pregnancies annually; and, 5,000 young people will commit suicide this year. Why?

Many suffer from what Dr. Viktor Frankl refers to as an "existential vacuum." It means that we have no instinct left to tell us what to do; we have no traditions left to tell us what we ought to do; and, many of us don't even know what we want to do. Consequently, many of us--especially teenagers--want to do what others are doing; or worse, we do what they want us to do.

A study of 7,948 students at 48 colleges and universities across the country revealed that 78% of them were looking for a purpose in life. Many of us don't know what we want in life, but we're fairly sure we don't have it.

WHY?

Could it be that parents aren't providing the correct type and amount of guidance and leadership? Could it be that some parents aren't even around? Could it be that some parents are, instead, abusing their children? In other words, could it be that parents aren't providing excellence in customer service to their kids?

I believe that when two adults decide to bring children into this world, they should concurrently assume the responsibility to ensure that their offspring are nurtured, guided, loved, and disciplined. It is their responsibility to create a well-rounded human being who can contribute something positive to this world.

NO PLANNING

Isn't it strange that we spend more time planning ski trips and summer vacations than we spend planning our families? With the advent of all the birth-control methods that we enjoy, there is little excuse for making a "mistake" and bringing an unplanned child into this world. And there is even less excuse for guys going around impregnating unsuspecting girls.

There should, of course, be severe penalties for such occurrences, for both sexes. There are very few guys today who don't know what "no" means.

NARCISSISM

Today, we live in a narcissistic society. We have become preoccupied with self-gratification and self-indulgence (I don't care about anyone else; if it feels good, do it). We have succumbed to hot-tub groupies, designer jeans for tots, too many Christmas presents, and an over-emphasis on youth, beauty, and sexuality. We want things to adorn, places to visit--not to share with others, but to show to others.

Denis Waitley says, "The single greatest cause of what's ailing America today is our irresponsible obsession with immediate sensual gratification. We want love without commitment, and benefits without production. Pain, effort and sacrifice are unacceptable. We're programmed to be entertained and are pacified by fun."

Author and speaker Jim Rohn says, "Failure is as predictable as success. The inability to delay gratification is a primary predictor of economic failure in life."

Too many people do what is fun and easy, rather than what is difficult and necessary. Psychoanalyst Aaron Stern states, "To attain emotional maturity, we must learn to develop two critical capacities: 1) the ability to live with uncertainty, and 2) the ability to delay gratification in favor of long-term goals."

Stern goes on to say, "Adolescence is time of maximum resistance to further growth. It is characterized by the teenager's ingenious efforts to maintain the privileges of childhood, while at the same time demanding the rights of adulthood."

IT'S OUR FAULT

I believe that we are raising a privileged society. More and more, we reward our children with material things and payoffs as a consequence of their mere "being there," rather than for their contributions to society. The more we do for our kids, the less they can do for themselves. Remember: "The dependent child of today will be the dependent parent of tomorrow."

Numerous young adults maturing today have been led to believe by their parents and the media that pain is unacceptable and that stress can be cured in 60 seconds. Guess what? They are going to have trouble coping with the real world.

Some of the biggest mistakes parents make is acting inconsistently and failing to set limits on demands. How is a child supposed to know how to act and what is to be expected of him if his "leader" constantly vacillates? How is a child going to be prepared to face life's problems when they occur if she has no reference point from which to operate?

As a whole, we adults have abdicated. We have capitulated. We have "thrown in the towel." We are letting little kids "run the show" and consequently, run our lives.

Why? Because it's easier that way. Take 'em to the baby sitter. Let 'em watch the tube. Ignore 'em when they have questions or when they want to play. It's our fault--not theirs.

Where in the world did we ever get the idea that a child has all the facts, experience, and knowledge needed to make tough decisions regarding sex, religion and personal relationships? They need our guidance. They need our help. They need our discipline.

Anything less is a gross disservice to the very kids that we profess to love. It's lousy customer service.

FATHERS ARE THE WORST

As reported by the Associated Press in the January 19, 1995, issue of the San Antonio Express-News, preschoolers worldwide spend less than one waking hour a day alone with their fathers, according to an 11-nation study. It goes on to say that mothers remain the primary adult in a preschooler's life, even when she works outside the home and the child is in day care.

The study, conducted by the International Association for the Evaluation of Educational Achievement, correctly concludes that fathers can hardly claim their limited solo performance is mitigated by the hours their children spend with both parents together. (That is, of course, assuming that the fathers in question are indeed around at all. Many shun their responsibilities and flee at the first sign of responsibility). See Figure 11-1.

Figure 11-1

Spending Time With Dad

Country	Time with Dad	Time in Day Care
Belgium	30 minutes	6.8 hours
China	54 minutes	11 hours
Finland	48 minutes	6.8 hours
Germany	36 minutes	5 hours
Hong Kong	6 minutes	3.4 hours
Italy	NA	7.2 hours
Nigeria	42 minutes	7 hours
Portugal	24 minutes	8.8 hours
Spain	18 minutes	7 hours
Thailand	12 minutes	11 hours
United States	42 minutes	5.6 hours

Source: *San Antonio Express-News*

WHAT'S THE ANSWER?

Provide love, understanding, guidance, training, and discipline. Responsibilities should be established for each member of the family--including the parents. Rules should be set in advance, and then abide by them. Be consistent in your demands and discipline. Nothing is more devastating than vacillation. How is a child to know what is expected if there is no consistency?

Until your kids reach the age to leave home, it is your right and your duty to know:

a. Where they are.
b. Who they are with.
c. What they're doing.
d. When they'll be home.

Be a role model for them. Don't preach what you don't practice. It's awfully difficult to convince your child that she should attend Sunday school while you sit home on Sunday mornings reading the paper. If, on the other hand, you've made a commitment that you can't meet, tell them why--and don't make excuses.

Teach your kids that life is a "do-it-yourself" project. Don't do everything for them. (This is a mistake our government is making with perpetual welfare recipients. They continue to get something for nothing and it is ruining them psychologically). But let your children know they can make honest mistakes without fear of punishment or rejection.

TRACTOR STORY

This is a true story. It happened to me a long time ago, but I'll never forget it as long as I live. I guess one could say my dad practiced excellence in customer service that day long ago.

I actively helped my dad on the farm since I could walk, and by the age of ten I had helped him with the planting, cultivating, and plowing. Operating the tractor was an enjoyable experience for me, and this was such a time.

It was time to cultivate the crops. The grain sorghum had tiptoed up several inches in height and its leaves were reaching out toward the heavens as if drawn by an unseen force. Unfortunately, so were the weeds.

Cultivating a field is similar to hoeing a garden, except it is done with sweeps or shovels bolted to a frame, which is attached to a tractor. As the tractor rolls along the rows, weeds are cut and swept out, while simultaneously, fresh soil is gently tossed around the stalks of the sorghum. This action causes the soil to be aerated, the slender stalks bolstered, and weeds eliminated--several rows at a time.

Dad had taught me carefully and expected me to follow his instructions meticulously. As I reached the end of the row, I was supposed to stop, lift the cultivator out of the ground by utilizing a hydraulic lever, turn around into the next set of rows, stop once again, lower the cultivator into the ground using the same lever, and proceed in the opposite direction. The procedure was simple enough, but to a ten-year-old boy, it seemed awfully slow and unchallenging.

In typical ten-year-old infinite-wisdom-fashion, I envisioned a new time-saving, although more challenging, procedure. The entire operation would be much more efficient if, instead of stopping at the end of each row, I would simultaneously trip the hydraulic lever, turn, once again trip the lever and proceed in the opposite direction--all in one fluid motion with no stops.

It was time to test my theory. I was as excited as I would later in life be on my first date. Besides, Dad was at the far end of the field about a half-mile away and probably wouldn't notice the fact that I had slightly altered his recommended procedure.

I came to the end of the row. I tripped the lever--or at least I thought I did. I turned--well, partially. Oh yes, one more thing. Did I mention the fence at the end of the rows? In a nutshell, the tractor's engine died, the cultivator became a pretzel, and the fence somehow jumped onto the tractor and was lovingly embracing it. And me? I was crying because I knew what was about to happen.

Dad was at the far end of the field--looking, looking, and looking. Then, in a flash, he jumped into his pickup truck and was heading my way.

As the clouds of dust chased the truck across the field, I experienced a variety of emotions. On the one hand, I was wishing he would never get there, and yet I wanted it to be over in a hurry. I had a sinking feeling that this whole sorry incident was about to result in a belt-loosening experience.

The truck screeched to a halt as a cloud of dust enveloped us. Tears were running down my cheeks and my self-esteem was lower than that of a barnyard mouse. Dad sauntered over toward me and carefully assessed the situation, and although it didn't take very long for him to ascertain what had happened, it seemed like an eternity to me.

Then a miracle happened. He put his hand on my shoulder and said, "It's okay, son. You just made a mistake." Some mistake!

He could have shouted, yelled, or screamed, "You idiot! Why don't you ever listen? Why didn't you do what I told you?" He could have destroyed what little self-esteem I had at that point.

How many of us have done just that? Help tear down our kids' self-esteem? But he just said, "It's okay, son. You just made a mistake." I'm not sure, but I believe he actually smiled a little bit. I will never forget how he picked me up that day, instead of squashing me down.

On that day long ago, in the middle of our field, I learned a valuable lesson: Allow mistakes; don't be afraid of making a few yourself; forgive others; and, forgive yourself.

The tractor? Dad still has it, even after all these years. Sometimes when I visit my folks out near Hondo, Texas, I sneak out to the shed and dust off my old friend.

TOUGH CHOICES-GREAT REWARDS

Parents simply cannot carry on business as usual when raising children. Disability leave and day care won't be enough. Your kids need health care and preschools, but most important, they need parental time and attention.

I'm sure you've heard the old familiar cop-out: "I make sure that the little time I spend with my child is quality time." The truth is: there is no quality time without quantity time! Time and time again, research has shown that there is a direct link between absentee parents and their kids' emotional and behavioral problems.

This is your chance to make a positive difference in the world. One of the noblest causes you can subscribe to is the creation and nurturing of solid, well-rounded children. If you don't want to make the necessary sacrifices to do so, let me suggest that you seriously consider not having kids. Our society is already reeling from the negative effects of rotten kids whose parents didn't care enough.

CASE IN POINT

In March of 1995, 17-year-old Bobby Vasquez was caught at 2:45 a.m. scrawling graffiti on the walls of a San Antonio nightclub. He was subsequently shot and killed for his actions.

Now, while most of us would agree that killing someone for scribbling something on a wall is hardly justified, there seems to be major disagreement over who ultimately bears the responsibility for this young man's death. Family and friends blamed the city because it "failed to provide activities for disadvantaged youths like Vasquez."

No one knew why Vasquez was out on the streets so late, but, continued his friends, "If they had activities, they would be too tired to get into mischief." Do you buy that?

As a matter of fact, the City of San Antonio does provide a variety of programs designed to help keep young people out of trouble, and Vasquez had played in a midnight basketball league for at-risk kids. Some say he died because he didn't have enough to do.

Whoa! Isn't it time to mention something revolutionary? Like parental responsibility? Isn't it time that we all take responsibility for our own actions and stop blaming everything and everybody else?

Vasquez's mother is single - wherein lies a huge problem that permeates the entire country. That's another whole subject beyond the scope of this book. Nevertheless, mothers and fathers, single mothers, and single fathers must be responsible for the actions of their kids until they are mature enough to be responsible for their own actions. Had that been the case here, Vasquez would still be alive today.

Remember, your kids are merely an extension of you. Be of service to them. Don't ignore 'em. Because if you do, they'll act just like a customer and silently go away.

Take a moment to listen today
to what your children are trying to say
Listen today, whatever you do
Or they won't be there to listen to you.
Listen to their problems, listen to their needs
Praise their smallest triumphs, praise their smallest deeds
Encourage their chatter, amplify their laughter
Find out what they're after, find out what's the matter.

Tell 'em that you love them each and every night
and even when you scold them, tell them they're all right
Because, you see, if we tell them all the bad in them we see
They'll grow up exactly like we hoped they'd never be.

But if we tell them that we're proud to share their name
They'll grow up believing that they're winners in life's game

So, take a moment to listen today
To what your children are trying to say
Listen today, whatever you do
And they'll be back to listen to you.

12

IT'S BEEN SAID BEFORE.

For almost five years, I had the privilege of writing a Sunday column for several newspapers. Entitled "A BREATH OF FRESH AIR," it was upbeat, positive, and sometimes, educational.

Numerous subjects were discussed, but none more than that of customer service. I felt this subject was so important that I slipped in a pertinent column whenever I could.

This chapter consists of 10 of my columns on customer service. They appear just as they did in the newspapers.

LIP SERVICE OR CUSTOMER SERVICE?

Customer service is not a competitive edge; it's THE competitive edge.

Since most of us are involved directly or indirectly with providing a service to customers, it is appropriate that we discuss one of the most important subjects of today--CUSTOMER SERVICE. Unfortunately, it is also one of the most frequently ignored aspects of doing business.

Signs, banners, slogans, and clever media ads inundate walls and airwaves, but too often, real service succumbs to only lip service. Frequently, we enter a business establishment or governmental office seeking help, only to be treated rudely, or even worse--ignored.

Two-thirds of this country's population is currently engaged in some aspect of the service industry. By the year 2000, approximately eighty-eight percent will be; hence, one of the reasons I receive an increasing number of requests to speak and to conduct seminars on the subject.

In a service-related industry, we never get a second chance to make a good first impression; and that first impression, known as a "moment of truth," occurs whenever a customer comes in contact with any aspect of your organization. It can occur over the phone, when a letter is opened, or when a customer enters your place of business.

No one is immune. Everyone should be concerned--from front-line personnel to the chairman of the board. If your total organization's culture doesn't show that service is the most important thing you offer the customer, then it isn't.

Unless the shared values, norms, beliefs, and ideologies of your organization are clearly and consciously focused on servicing the customer, there is little chance that your organization will be able to deliver a consistent quality of service and to develop a sustained reputation for service.

Historically, customer service was relegated to a "customer service" department, thereby inferring that no one else needed to be concerned. We must, however, all be interested in serving the customer; and if you're not directly serving the customer, you had better be serving someone who is.

There are three general stages of business failure:

Stage 1: We'll do anything for the customer. (Usually occurs when a business opens).

Stage 2: We're too busy. (Usually occurs when business is so good that we simply don't have time to worry about every customer).

Stage 3: We'll do anything for the customer. (Usually occurs after it's too late to make any difference).

When "moments of truth" go unmanaged, quality of service regresses to mediocrity. John Naisbett, in his book Re-Inventing the Corporation, says, "People don't buy things; they buy expectations. The more we face 'high tech' the more we want 'high touch.'"

CUSTOMERS MAKE PROFITS

How would you like to live in a country where everyone votes? Wouldn't that be exciting?

You do, in fact, live in such a country. Every day everyone votes with their dollars--for you or for your competitor.

I recently had the privilege of addressing a group of customer service experts at the 12th Annual Conference of the International Customer Service Association. Over 1,000 attendees from the U.S., Canada, and Great Britain descended upon San Antonio to learn and share ideas about improving customer service within their respective companies.

Unless everyone--from the CEO to the front line employee--becomes obsessed with customer service and satisfaction, your company will race toward oblivion. Unfortunately, only about five percent of all companies in the U.S. are engaged in providing exceptional customer service; the other 95 percent are paying only lip service.

In a service environment where 68 percent of your customers who leave do so because of an attitude problem on the part of someone in your company, isn't it time to look around to see who might be causing the problem? Could it be you?

You might be thinking that this subject is directed solely at business owners and corporate officers, but nothing could be further from the truth. We should all be interested in providing excellent customer service; our companies and our jobs just might depend on it.

But, you reason, "I'm not directly serving the customer." Tom Peters reminds us in Thriving on Chaos that if we are not serving the customer directly, then we had better be serving someone who is.

USAA's Beverly McClure compares the service situation to a chain. She says, "We're only as effective as the weakest link."

So, no matter what your job is--even if you are an accountant, engineer, teacher, lawyer, or bank president--you are in the chain that delivers customer satisfaction--or dissatisfaction. Make yours the strongest link.

Generally speaking, companies that are perceived as providing excellent customer service will out perform their rivals by a two-to-one margin. They will average a twelve percent return on sales; their rivals, one percent. They will gain a six percent market share each year; their rivals will lose two percent. Where would you rather be?

You can make the difference. You can change your attitude if needed. You can start the move in your company to a new outlook toward serving customers.

BECOME USER FRIENDLY

"Customer service is not a competitive edge; it is the competitive edge"--Karl Albrecht in Service America.

Ever so often, I feel compelled to dedicate a column to the subject of customer service. I believe that the term "customer service" is the most misused, misinterpreted, and misunderstood term in the business world.

Everyone professes a belief in the need for excellent customer service. Yet, only five percent of companies and organizations in this country actually practice it. The rest only practice lip service.

My soon to-be-published book, Don't Shoot the Customer, as well as my seminar by the same title, focuses on the importance of providing excellent customer service. One out of four of your customers are unhappy enough to leave you, and 90 percent of those will. Worse yet, they will tell ten others about the poor service they have received.

It costs six times more to attract new customers than to keep existing ones. Customer service used to be regarded as an expense, as a necessary evil. However, we now know that excellent customer service actually increases sales while reducing the cost of sales.

Fred Smith, founder of Federal Express, states, "The U.S. has been terrible as it applies to customer service. I mean we killed the goose that laid the golden egg. Somehow, management let employees believe that customers weren't important."

How you think you are being perceived and how you are actually being perceived can be worlds apart. For example, how would you like to deal with a company that utilizes a snobby receptionist, last names only when conversing in front of clients, and a telephone system that bores you with incessant self-praise while you languish "on hold." I thought so.

Or how about a clerk who keeps you waiting while she finishes an animated conversation with her boyfriend on the phone? Or a banker who makes you squirm while you beg for a loan? (Remember, they need to lend money; they are the seller and you are the buyer).

If you serve the public, remember: your job and your organization exist because of and for the customer. If your organization's culture doesn't show that service is the most important thing you offer, then it isn't.

If you are a customer, remember: You don't have to put up with companies and organizations which aren't "user friendly." They deserve to fail.

CUSTOMERS? WHO ARE THEY?

"If you're not serving the customer, you'd better be serving someone who is." - Ron Zempke, in his book, *Service America!*

Typical business organizations pay the least attention to their front-line people--sales clerks, receptionists, and cashiers. These jobs usually get the least pay, the least training and development, and the least gratitude. Consequently, these people, in many cases, also exhibit the least motivation, the least loyalty, and the most turnover.

Is it their fault? Of course not! We spend enormous amounts of money advertising to lure customers into our front door. But that all evaporates the minute the customer encounters a non-supportive front-line employee.

Poorly trained front-liners usually have little choice but to develop their own methods of selling and servicing. Unfortunately, most of their methods don't work very well.

Customer retention is closely tied to employee effectiveness. How customers feel about the people who service them is a vital factor in winning and keeping them, so it behooves everyone to support those front-liners who have direct contact with customers.

Janet Rush, co-founder of Strawberry Communications, in her recent seminar in San Antonio, asked the question, "Who is your internal customer?" even before she asked, "Who is your external customer?" She went on to say, "A customer is anyone who can influence a sale, a vote, a budget, a job, or a career."

"In other words," Janet reminded us, "almost everyone with whom we come in contact is a potential customer. The list includes employees, your boss, your spouse, your kids, relatives, and friends."

It's safe to say that everyone in a sales or service organization has a service role, even those who never see the ultimate customer. Included are supervisors, managers, accountants, and even executives.

If your organization's culture doesn't show that service is the most important thing you can offer the customer, then it isn't. Furthermore, the organization exists to support those who serve the customer.

The concept of customer service is so vital that, as a public service, the San Antonio Express-News will be offering, for a nominal fee, a customer service learning shop in February, with the exact date to be announced later. I will have the pleasure of conducting the seminar and look forward to sharing ideas, experiences, and proven precepts with you.

Entitled, "DON'T SHOOT THE CUSTOMER," this half-day experience will not only tickle your funny bone, but it will also provide tangible "meat and potatoes" concepts that attendees can take with them and put into practice. More information will be forthcoming in future columns.

"GOOD ENOUGH" NEVER IS

Quality must be judged as the customer perceives it. Specifications should define what it takes to satisfy--no, to pleasantly surprise, the customer.

Fred Smith, founder of Federal Express, declared, "The U.S. has been terrible as it applies to customer service. When the history of American business is written, I think that's going to be the most incredible part of what we did. I mean, we killed the goose that laid the golden egg. Somehow, management let employees believe that customers weren't important."

Studies show that 96 percent of those customers who have a bad experience fail to report it--at least not to the place where they had their bad experience. Why?

The reason is no surprise. They expect no satisfaction even if they do report it. Unfortunately, however, they will tell 10 other people about it.

How can we, as business owners, managers, government officials, educators, and professionals stem the tide? By LISTENING!

Listen frequently; listen systematically; listen openly. Absorb and pass information to its required destination--quickly and without distortion. How we think we are being perceived by the customer and how the customer actually perceives us can vary greatly.

It is not enough just to provide excellent service; our customers must perceive that they are getting excellent service. And, unless we become obsessed with really listening to complaints, as well as compliments, we will eventually crash and burn.

Of the customers who register a complaint, up to 70 percent will continue to do business with us if the complaint is resolved; up to 95 percent if the complaint is resolved quickly. Some become even more loyal than they were in the first place.

In order to receive complaints, however, we must make it easy for customers to complain. Become "transparent" to customers by using the ears of everyone in your organization. Encourage feedback; engage in dialogue; flee your desk and walk the front lines. Practice some "visible management."

How is your organization doing? Have you personally become involved in customer service, or is your firm merely displaying flashy banners, cute buttons, and catchy slogans?

Or do you care? If you happen to be the only organization of your type in town, please don't act like it. Humanity is only as good as its weakest element. Don't let it be you.

Are your front-line employees obsessed with customer service or only with "quittin' time?" Do you trust your employees with your survival?

BE A PRO

We're the PRO's and should be the CEO's.

Even though my background is in management, and although some classify me as a motivational speaker, I harbor some doubts as to whether or not any person can truly motivate another.

To be sure, most us can be extremely motivated by fear or by euphoria for short periods of time, but long-term motivation must originate from within oneself. In order to accomplish that, one must have reference points from which to begin.

I believe as I frequently declare, especially in addresses to teachers and parents, that the adult community has the awesome Privilege, Responsibility, and Opportunity to make a real difference in our young people's lives--establishing reference points. We are the PRO's.

We have the ability to set the example and to provide the guidance our young people so desperately need today.

A similar phenomenon exists in the business world--"visible management." Tom Peters, in his book Thriving on Chaos, says, "Visible management is a requisite today. To enable all organization members to get comfortable with change and constant risk-taking, management must be ever present--training, coaching, cajoling, caring, and comforting."

He goes on to emphasize, "You are out of tune with the times if you are in the office more than one-third of the time."

One can conclude that, similarly, if we are out of touch with our children too much of the time, our communication channels with them will eventually be cut. Chaos and anarchy will follow.

So, why not pattern your family unit somewhat like you would a business? Practice "visible management." Be in touch so they'll stay in touch.

Become a CEO:

Communicate--don't vacillate
Educate--don't vegetate
Officiate--don't abdicate

Listen to their problems; share their joys; know their friends. We have the power and authority to manage our family units, and it is incumbent upon us to use it wisely.

Perhaps the most important work project we will ever accomplish in our lives is the molding of our children so they have a chance to become worthwhile adults--just like us.

Our children mirror our philosophies. They think like us, look like us, act like us--they are like us.

What do you see? Achievement or failure? Happiness or depression? Optimism or despair? Start today practicing "visible management."

We are the Pro's and should be the CEO's.

CUSTOMER SERVICE DOESN'T COST

Last week we spoke about the absolute need for providing excellent customer service. All of us should be interested--business people, doctors, lawyers, educators, government employees, and public officials--everybody.

Why is customer service so important? Because one out of four clients, patients, or customers is unhappy enough to leave you. Unfortunately, ninety percent (of the one out of four) will.

Displeased clients, patients, or customers will express their displeasure to ten others. To make matters worse, it costs six times more to attract new business as it does to retain old business.

Why is it that salespeople are paid more to attract new business than to maintain what they already have? It doesn't make sense.

Customer service used to be regarded as an expenditure. Now, we know that it increases sales and decreases their cost.

How do we know? Businesses, with a perceived low quality of service, average one percent return on sales. Those with a perceived high quality of service average twelve percent return.

Additionally, low quality service businesses annually lose two percent of their market share. Those with high quality service gain six percent per year.

The aforementioned statistics would have to attract the attention of even the most hardened individuals. Service doesn't cost--it pays.

Let me share with you a poignant recollection that many of you have probably experienced.

I recently entered a restaurant, was brusquely ushered to a table, and began my vigil. No one offered me a glass of water, nor even a menu. A couple that arrived later had their order taken first.

Did I complain? No. I don't believe in that sort of thing. Just because the restaurant personnel were rude, doesn't mean I had to be. I left, still hungry. No one noticed.

Later, I went to a leading sports outlet. A female clerk snapped, "Yeah?" I almost forgot what I was there for, but quickly recovered with a cheerful, "Good morning!"

"Humph!" she sputtered. "What d 'ya need?" Suddenly, I decided that I didn't need anything after all.

My last stop for the day was at my bank. I had a question concerning additional charges that appeared on my statement. The young lady had no idea what the charges meant, but fully agreed with me that things were really messed up. I transferred my account and no one ever asked why.

I don't like to complain. I never raise a ruckus. Just because I'm treated badly, or ignored, doesn't mean I have to create a scene.

Do you know who I am? I'm the nice customer. I'm also the customer who NEVER COMES BACK.

SERVICE EQUALS SURVIVAL

Rewarded customers will buy, notify, and multiply!

We have recently reviewed the absolute necessity of providing excellent customer service:

1. It increases sales and reduces their cost.
2. It increases market share.

What better reasons could there be to hone your skills in the art of customer service?

Okay, let's assume you agree. How can we go about instilling this philosophy throughout our businesses, schools, professions, and governments?

First, establish a mission statement. What do you stand for? What makes your organization unique? How are you doing so far?

Conducting reliable market research, properly analyzing the data, and training your personnel accordingly constitute the first steps toward establishing your market strategy. Now you are ready to position yourself in the marketplace and provide direction for your organization.

To survive and prosper requires differentiation. "Average" equals "mediocrity."

The second major consideration in the customer service arena is, of course, the customer. According to psychologists, a person is capable of experiencing four basic emotions: scared, sad, mad, and glad. As one might guess, customers will respond favorably only if they are in a glad mood.

We are ruled by our emotions. We base nearly all our choices on how we feel about a situation. Consequently, it is in our best interest to cause our customers to be happy.

The third major ingredient of an effective customer service program is the employee. Customer retention is closely tied to employee effectiveness, as well as to employee retention.

How customers feel about the people who serve them is a key factor in winning them and keeping them. After all, in many cases, the receptionist, the clerk, or the salesperson, "is" the company.

Furthermore, customers are far more impressed by the depth of your beliefs and emotions than by any amount of knowledge or logic you possess. The greatest customer you'll ever win is you.

Any program for maximum employee effectiveness should include the following:

1. A motivating environment - encouraging a well-balanced life, a high energy level, and a sense of optimism.
2. Effective people - possessing high self-esteem, adequate social skills, and a tolerance for human contact.
3. Empowerment - granting front-line personnel the authority to do whatever it takes to meet, or exceed, the customer's expectations.

4. Total management commitment that will train 'em well, pay 'em well, and support 'em well.

We all ultimately work for our customers - whether we are business people, doctors, lawyers, teachers, government employees, or union workers - all of us.

Excellent service is not merely a competitive weapon. It's a survival skill.

THE GOVERNMENT'S CUSTOMERS

"Quality may be the biggest competitive issue of the late 20th and 21st Centuries."
- Stephen Shepard, Editor-in-Chief, *Business Week*

I would feel remiss if I didn't take time to thank the 600-plus participants of my March 2nd customer service seminar, "Don't Shoot the Customer," and its spin-off sessions.

Also, I want to publicly express my gratitude to the San Antonio Express-News for its sponsorship and support. It's this very type of public service that has propelled this newspaper into its dominant position in the marketplace.

It is also this kind of customer/public service attitude that can help ensure not only your survival, but also extraordinary success in your business. Being a good corporate citizen is as important as being a good private citizen.

Despite the fact that some may be intimidated by its terminology, requirements, and procedures, customer service, and its systems counterpart - Total Quality Management (TQM)--both begin with a change in attitude. Both are dependent on total management commitment--top to bottom.

Unless your organization's culture demonstrates that quality customer products and services are the most important products that you offer--then they aren't. You are providing lip service, not customer service. And all the buttons, banners, and cute slogans won't cover up the stench.

Whether it's corporate, professional, or individual, serving humankind constitutes one of the noblest undertakings in which we can become involved. In all cases, inspiring people to think differently, and to do things differently, takes leaders who can communicate what needs to be done and why.

It takes leaders who have a clear vision or goal, can impart that vision to others, and then demonstrate through action how to make the vision a reality. Wouldn't it be refreshing to see our political leaders practice these precepts for a change?

Dr. Robert Anthony, in his book Total Self-Confidence, reminds us that every person is an extension of everyone else. He says that we must make it our personal responsibility to elevate the consciousness of humankind for, like a chain, the human race is only as strong as its weakest link.

So, let's cut out the funny stuff. I challenge corporations to study, learn, and practice true customer service and total quality management. It's your only hope for survival and success.

I challenge politicians to study, learn, and practice true public service. It's your only hope of returning our nation back to the principles on which it was founded (and it might help you get re-elected, too).

I challenge everyone to study, learn, and practice true service to humankind. Get off the couch, turn off the TV, and become involved with your schools, neighborhoods, and kids. It's the only way to prevent a few political, bureaucratic, and social misfits from ruining our country and our lives.

KIDS "R" CUSTOMERS

Recently, I dialed a bank's telephone number and was promptly relegated to second-class status by a recording. In a squeaky, non-personal voice it recited, "You have reached XYZ Bank. If you need accounting, dial ONE now. If you need consumer loans, dial TWO now. If you need customer service, dial THREE now."

You gotta be kidding! CUSTOMER SERVICE? A recording?

Ron Zempke, in his book Service America!, declares, "The more we are faced with high tech, the more we want high touch." In other words, consumers are fed up with being treated like numbers, instead of as people.

Warren Blanding, editor and publisher of "Customer Service Newsletter," suggests: "The trend toward consumerism and the changing competitive climate have forced companies to reexamine their relationships with customers. As a result, customer service has become a strategic tool."

Harvard Business School Professor Theodore Lewitt likens the relationship between today's buyer and seller to a marriage. "The era of the one-night stand is gone," he says.

Yet the great majority of corporations today don't practice effective customer service--only lip service. Unfortunately for them, however, the public has become wiser. It warns: "What you are speaks so loudly, I can't hear what you're saying."

Buttons, slogans, and glib TV ads simply don't cut it anymore. In other words, if you don't really mean what you say, don't say it.

The same principle holds true in our family lives. Many of us suffer from Jones-phobia and, consequently, pay only scant attention to the needs and wants of our most important customers--our spouses and children.

Because of economic pressures, many of us are chasing our tails to nowhere. We simply run out of time and energy by the time we arrive home each evening.

So, instead of sharing quality time with our kids, we rationalize by professing how our hard work demonstrates our love for them. But after a while, they stop listening and we suddenly discover one day that they grew up while we were away at work.

Then, when it's too late, we realize that we have been giving lip service--not providing real service--to our family. The results are predictable; they drift away.

Just as our business customers abandon us when we start taking them for granted, so do our loved ones. And we have the audacity to ask, "What happened?"

We piously mutter, "We've done everything for them. They had everything they ever wanted." (Except our time, patience, understanding, empathy, and love).

Just like business customers, our families don't care how much we know until they know how much we care.

CONCLUSION

Well, what do you think? Are you ready to hang up your pistols and arm yourself with a renewed determination to improving your customer service attitude? It's a mindset, you know.

You must become obsessed with it. You must be consistent. You must be persistent. Why? Because your co-workers, employees, and friends are likely to take pot-shots at your new-found program.

You can - no, you must prevail. Dodge the bullets of doubt, skepticism, and cynicism. Just because others tried and gave up, doesn't mean you can't succeed.

Sure, it's difficult. Yes, there are barriers. Of course, there will be problems. Not everyone will buy into the customer service concept--at least not right away.

Chip away at resistance. Take small steps at first, even if it's your company, or your students, or your children, or your civil servants.

It's even more difficult if you are working from the bottom instead of the top, but you can still do it. Set the example. Start with your own area--but START.

Appendix I

SURVEY PARTICIPANTS

AAA Potomac

Cecilia Quattromani, Manager - Member Relations
12600 Fair Lakes Circle, Fairfax, VA 22033-4904

Amoco Oil Company

Rudy Marcinko, Manager - Customer Support Service
4300 Westown Parkway, Des Moines, IA 50265

Anheuser-Busch Distributors of New York, Inc.

Terri DeToli, Customer Service Coordinator
55-01 Second Street, Long Island City, NY 11101

Atlantic Region Management Training Center

Laura Boyd-Brown, Consultant and Trainer
1340 Barrington St., P.O. Box 1000, Halifax, Novia Scotia 2x4

AT&T Global Consumer Communications Services

George D. Harris, National Sales Director
3A06 One Speedwell Ave., Morristown, N.J. 07960

Baptist Hospital of Miami

Helen C. DeSautel, R.N., M.S., Director, Patient/Guest Services
8900 North Kendall Drive, Miami, FL 33176-2197

Bass Pro Shops

Arley M. Clark, Director of Catalog Services
1935 S. Campbell, Springfield, MO 65898

Bay State Gas Company

Kim Corwin, Director - Human Resources & Corporate Performance
300 Friberg Parkway, Hestborough, MA

Baskin-Robbins

Kathie Bellamy, Manager - Consumer Affairs
31 Baskin-Robbins Place, Glendale, CA 91202

Belhouth Corporation

Bill McCloskey, Director - Media Relations

Beltone Electronics
Janet C. Nicholson, Manager - Customer Service
4201 W. Victoria Street, Chicago, IL 60646

Ben and Jerry's Homemade, Inc.
Alice C. Blachly, Consumer Affairs Coordinator
Route 100, P.O. Box 240, Waterbury, VT 05676

Bil Mar Foods, Inc.
Stephen Twenney, Director, Sales and Marketing Services
8300 96th Ave., Zeeland, MI 49464-0305

BMW Center
J. M. Carnes, President
4623 Fredericksburg, San Antonio, TX 78201

British Airways
Helen Camera, Manager - Customer Relations & Refunds, USA
75-20 Asteria Blvd, Jackson Heights, NY

Broadway National Bank
Charles E. Cheever, Jr., Chairman
P.O. Box 1701, San Antonio, TX 78286

Brown and Sharpe Manufacturing Company
Penny Panebianco, Customer Service Supervisor
Precision Park, North Kingstown, RI 02852

Budget Rent-A-Car Corporation
Kathy Lowry, Supervising Manager, Customer Relations
P.O. Box 111580, Carrollton, TX 75011-1580

Children's National Medical Center
Barbara A. Cady, Director - Physician Relations
Medical Center, 111 Michigan Ave., N.W., Washington, D.C.

Cadillac Motor Car Company
John W. Hautman, Director - Consumer Relations
2860 Clark Street, Detroit, MI 48232

Coca-Cola Bottling Company of New York, Inc.
Harriet Tolve, Consumer Affairs Manager
20 Horseneck Lane, Greenwich, CT 06830

Commonwealth Edison Company
William H. Downey, VP - Customer Operations
P.O. Box 767-37FNW, Chicago, IL 60690

Consolidated Rail Corporation
Paul J. Hiryak, Director - Employee Development & Customer Service Admin.
P.O. Box 41408, Customer Service Department, 8-A 2001 Market Street
Philadelphia, PA 19101-1408

The Consumer Voice
Carol D. Scroggins, President
3441 W. Memorial Rd., Suite 8, Oklahoma City, OK 73134

Continental Airlines San Antonio
Joseph Delpero, General Manager
9700 Airport Blvd, San Antonio, TX 78216

The Copps Corporation
Judy Ordens, Director of Consumer Affairs
2828 Wayne St., Stevens Point WI 54481

Corning Consumer Products Company
Linda L. McIntyre, Manager
1300 Hopeman Parkway, Waynesboro, VA 22980

Credit Data Southwest, Inc.
Aaron Huber, Manager - Consumer Assistance
706 North 1st St., Phoenix, AZ 58004-2011

CVC Products, Inc.

Marilee Masi, Manager - Order Service
525 Lee Road, Rochester, NY 14603

Cy Decosse, Inc.

Sherry Healy, Manager - Customer Service
5900 Green Oak Drive, Minnetonka, MN 55343-9692

Day Runner, Inc.

David McDaniel, Customer Service Manager
2750 W. Moore Ave., Fullerton, CA 92633

Diamond Shamrock, Inc.

R.R. Hemminghaus, Chairman, CEO, & President
P.O. Box 696000, San Antonio, TX 78269-6000

Direct Marketing Association, Inc.

Chester G. Dalzell, Director - Public Relations/Communications
11 West 42nd St., New York, NY 10036-8096

Du Pont Company

Robert R. Baer, Systems Specialist
P.O. Box 80021, Wilmington, DE 19880-0021

Durand Research and Marketing Association

Judith Durand, Manager - Consumer Research

5614 Cerritos, Houston, TX 77035

Eberhard Faber Corporation

Ellen Ingram Crosslin, Senior Customer Service Representative
Nashville, TN

Federal Express Corporation

Jean H. Ward-Jones, Manager - Corporate Quality
P.O. Box 727, Memphis, TN 38194-2141

Ford Motor Company

Dale A. Burns, Owner Relations Manager
1455 Lincoln Parkway, Suite 440, Atlanta, GA 30346

General Mills, Inc. BCE

Beverly Chapple, Manger - Customer Service
13400 15th Avenue N., P.O. Box 118, Minnesota, MN 55440

Gerber Products Company

Rita Van Boven, Manager - Consumer Relations
Nancy Linder, Manager - Public Relations
445 State St., Fremont, MI 49412

Halo Distributing Company

Dennis Sean O'Malley, President
P.O. Box 7370, San Antonio, TX 78207

The H. R. Chally Group

Cheryl D. Gier, CEO and Director of Sales
500 Lincoln Park Blvd, Dayton, OH 45429

The Iams Company

Sally J. Northcutt, Manager - Customer Service
7250 Poe Ave., P.O. Box 14597, Dayton, OH

The John Henry Company

Shirley A. Fraser, Director of Customer Service
5800 West Grand River, P.O. Box 17099, Lansing, MI 48901

Kaset International

Juan F. Gutierrez, Sr. Vice President
8875 Hidden River Parkway, Suite 400, Tampa, FL 33637

King Soopers

Laurie Weisman, Manager - Customer Relations
65 Tejon St., Denver, CO 80223

KLM Royal Dutch Airlines
Hans Adama Van Scheltema, Director - Service
656 Taxtor Road, Elmsford, NY 10523

Lego Systems, Inc.
Lois B. Ritchotte, Senior Manager - Consumer Affairs
555 Taylor Road, P.O. Box 1600, Enfield, CT

Long Island Lighting Company
Judy Torres, Research Analyst
175 East Old Country Road, Hicksville, NY

Lysis Corporation
Charlotte Hixson, Director - Customer Support and Implementation
740 W. Peachtree St., Atlanta, GA 30308

Martiz
Marjorie Schwenk, Director - Business Planning & Expansion
14956 Manor Lake Dr., Chesterfield, MO

Marriott (San Antonio Rivercenter)
Walter Kennedy, Resident Manager
101 Bowie St., San Antonio, TX 78205

McCombs Enterprises
Red McCombs, Owner
P.O. Box BH003, San Antonio, 78201

McNeil Specialty Products Company
Carol Jean Stafford, Manager - Consumer Affairs
501 George St., New Brunswick, NJ 08903

Merrill Lynch (San Antonio)
Dick Meacham, Assistant Vice President
P.O. Box 795003, San Antonio 78279

Midas International
Louis Gergits, Manager - Consumer Relations
225 North Michigan Ave., Chicago, IL 60601

John Morrell and Company
Lori Sproat, Supervisor - Consumer Affairs
Chiquita Center - 9th Floor, 250 E. 5th St., Cincinnati, OH 45202

Mountain Fuel Supply Company
Carl B. Galbaraith, Director - Customer Support
180 East One Hundred South, Salt Lake City, UT 84139

Nikon, Inc.

Robi Martin, General Manager - Customer Relations
19601 Hamilton Ave., Torrance, CA 90502

Our Lady of the Lake University

Elizabeth Anne Sueltenfull, President
411 S.W. 24th St., San Antonio 78207-4666

Promus Hotels

Pat R. Ferguson, Vice President - Human Resources
1023 Cherry Road, Memphis, TN 38117

Regal Ware, Inc.

Carol Heller, Manager - Consumer Services
1675 Reigle Dr., Kewaskum, WI 53040

San Antonio Express-News

W. Lawrence Walker, Jr., Publisher and CEO
P.O. Box 2171, San Antonio, TX 78297-2171

Shopsmith, Inc.

Dixie Moore, Consumer Relations Manager
3931 Image Dr., Dayton, OH 45414

SunService

Director - Customer Relations & Quality
2550 Garcia Ave., Mountain View, CA 94043-1100

Tetley Inc.

Ellen S. Horen, Manager - Consumer Affairs
100 Commerce Dr., Shelton, CT 06484

Whitehall-Robins

Marc J. Seim, Manager - Consumer Affairs
1405 Cummings Dr., Richmond, VA 23235

Note: 5 additional surveys were also submitted anonymously and several letters of regret were returned.

Appendix II

Permissions

Permission granted by CEO Howard Stevens, The H. R. Chally Group. Founded in 1973, Chally has become the technology leader in the assessment and prediction of sales, marketing, and management potential. With over 1,500 clients worldwide, its databases on methods and effectiveness include over 150,000 salespeople, 11,000 corporate customers, and 400 total sales forces. With corporate offices in Dayton, Ohio and Pacific Rim headquarters in Sydney Australia, Chally individually assesses and evaluates over 10,000 sales and management applicants a year.

Permission granted by Mr. T. R. Fehrenback to reprint his article entitled, "Too Much Worry Over Waning Species," as it appeared in the San Antonio Express-News, January 22, 1995.

Permission granted by Dr. Charles E. Gilliland, Associate Research Economist, Real Estate Center, Texas A&M University, to reprint his article entitled, "What's the Cost? Private Property, Public Use," as it appeared in the Tierra Grande Magazine, Summer 1994 issue.

Permission granted by Mary Jane Brukardt, Director of Communications, The Johnson Foundation, Racine, Wisconsin, to reprint various articles as they appeared in An American Imperative: Higher Expectations for Higher Education, 1993.

Permission granted by Technical Assistance Research Programs Institute, Arlington, Virginia, to reprint excerpts of various studies.

INDEX

Ken Nietenhoefer has become a sought after speaker and seminar leader for convention keynotes, corporate meetings, and after-dinner addresses - motivation, customer sevice, and student education. For additional information regarding availablity and fees, please call or write:

KCN COMMUNICATIONS
23567 IH 10 West
San Antonio, Texas 78257-9514
(210) 698-1702
1-800-992-2397

Partial List of KCN Clients:

American Heart Assoc.
AT&T Global Communications Solutions
American Telephone & Telegraph Co.
Boerne Independent School District
Builders Square
Builders, Owners, and Managers Assoc.
Cafe Lite & Bakery
Center for Aggregates Research
Central TX Society of Hosp. Pharmacists
Century 21 Real Estate
Compass Alliance Real Estate Services
Department of the Air Force
Dunhill Personnel
Duro Bag, Inc.
Hondo Independent School District
Incarnate Word College
International Customer Service Assoc.
Kelly Air Force Base
National Assoc. of Credit Managers
National Assoc. of Indpt. Resurfacers
Nation Assoc. of Realtors
National Assoc. of Women in Construction
National Cement Credit Division
Pioneer Hy-Bred
P.M.I. Mortgage Insurance Co.
Red Carpet Real Estate
San Antonio Board of Realtors
San Antonio Express-News
Society of Plastics Industries
South Texas Assoc. for Counseling & Dev.
Sonitrol National Dealers Assoc.
Southwest Texas State Univ.
Southwestern Bell Telephone
Texas A&M University
Texas Assoc. of Assessing Officers
Texas Chamber of Commerce
Texas Chiropractic Assoc.
Texas Circul. Mgt. Assoc.
Texas Education Agency
Texas Municipal League
Three Rivers Indep. School District
The Univ. of Texas at Austin
The Univ. of Texas San Antonio
USAA
Y's Men International
H.B. Zachry Company